I0983433

Indian
Wars *and* Warriors
East

Indian Wars *and* Warriors *East*

PAUL I. WELLMAN

Illustrated by Lorence Bjorklund

HOUGHTON MIFFLIN COMPANY BOSTON
The Riverside Press Cambridge

Books by

PAUL I. WELLMAN

Novels

Broncho Apache
Jubal Troop
Angel with Spurs
The Bowl of Brass
The Walls of Jericho
The Chain
The Iron Mistress
The Comancheros
The Female
Jericho's Daughters
Ride the Red Earth

Histories

Death on the Prairie
Death in the Desert
republished together as
The Indian Wars of the West
The Trampling Herd
Glory, God and Gold

Reminiscence

Portage Bay

For younger readers

Gold in California
Indian Wars and Warriors (East)
Indian Wars and Warriors (West)

LIBRARY OF CONGRESS CATALOG CARD NUMBER: 59-7473
THE RIVERSIDE PRESS
CAMBRIDGE · MASSACHUSETTS
PRINTED IN THE U.S.A.
Fourth Printing R

To

that wonderful lady, my aunt

M. Alice Isely

with whom, as a young lad, I

saw the West before it was

tamed, and who was never too

busy to help and guide me as

I gained my first deep taste

of its history.

CONTENTS

For almost three centuries the white man fought the Indian for possession of the North American continent. From 1609 when Champlain gave the Iroquois their first taste of gunfire until 1890 when the defeated Sioux laid down their arms, there was scarcely a year that did not see bloodshed.

Paul Wellman has written a brilliant, concise and fair-minded account of one of the longest wars in history. He has split his great subject into two fast-paced volumes: INDIAN WARS AND WARRIORS (EAST) AND INDIAN WARS AND WARRIORS (WEST). *The first of these two volumes—the one that you now hold in your hand—covers the long struggle on the eastern side of the Mississippi.*

No longer does the white man fear the scalping knife, the flaming arrow, or the dread war-cry of the attacking tribesman echoing from the forest. But the Indian, too, is safe at last from the armed white man seeking his extermination.

In the words of Abraham Lincoln, speaking of another conflict, let us view this struggle, "With malice toward none; with charity for all. . . ."

Sterling North
General Editor

Probable Location of
INDIAN TRIBES
of
EASTERN NORTH AMERICA
Before White Settlement
Montagnais
Abittibi
Nipissing
Malecite
Micmac
Abnaki
Passamaquoddy
Penobscot
Algonkin
Chippewa
Menomini
Winnebago
Sauk-Fox
Ottawa
Huron
Wyandot
Iroquois
Massachusetts
Pequot
Mahican
Narragansett
Forest Potawatomi
Neutrals
Munsee
Erie
Delaware
Iowa
Peoria
Piankashaw
Prairie Potawatomi
Susquehanna
Nanticoke
Miami
Kickapoo
Pamunkey
Mattapony
Illinois
Missouri
Shawnee
Powhatan
Tutelo
Osage
Tuscarora
Croatan
Catawba
Quapaw
Cherokee
Upper-Creek
Caddo
Chickasaw
Choctaw
Yuchi
Tunican
Lower-Creek
Natchez
Atakapa
Biloxi
Seminole
Apalachee
Timuquanan

Columbus Called Them "Indians"  1

ON THE TWELFTH DAY of October, in the year 1492, after a long voyage into the unknown, three small Spanish ships commanded by an Italian named Christopher Columbus splashed out anchors off a verdant island inhabited by a few brown-skinned natives.

Today we know it as Watlings Island, off the coast of Florida. But Columbus named it San Salvador, and believed he had reached the Indies, off the coast of Asia. At once he called the natives "Indians."

caught the imagination of the world.

By no means were they all alike. In the vast forests of the east, the Indians lived chiefly by hunting, though with some growing of corn, squash, and beans. Their dwellings were bark-roofed, and sometimes protected by palisades. They developed the light, graceful birch-bark canoe, their chief mode of transportation. Their hair they dressed in fantastic styles, warriors sometimes shaving the entire skull except for the "scalp lock," which was ornamented and feathered. Other fashions were to let the hair dangle loosely, or even to shave one side of the head

and let the hair on the other side grow long.

In the southern areas, agriculture was more extensive and the towns more permanent. Dwellings were thatched with matting, grass, or palmetto fronds. Here the pirogue, a canoe made of a hollowed log, was used.

Without exception Indians of all tribes were fond of decoration, painting their faces and bodies, wearing feathers, earrings, nose rings, and other adornments that often gave them a terrifying appearance.

A vast deal of nonsense has been written about Indian "kings," "queens," "princesses," and even "emperors." This arose out of the European's habit of thinking in such terms about his own rulers. Actually there never was an Indian king, in the true sense, within the area of the United States; and certainly no Indian princesses, romantic as that sounds.

Various names, such as *sagamore, sachem,* and *cacique* — all corruptions of Indian words — have been applied to Indian leaders. But the general term "chief," in the sense of a head man, is probably best. Chiefs often were temporary, but even when permanent they had no power of law to uphold them, relying on custom and personal influence for authority. Where a chief inherited his title, it usually was through his mother's side of the family.

Division of labor was a matter of physical ability. To women fell the tasks of the home, cooking, care of the children, garment making, gathering nuts and fruits, and simple gardening. To men went the hard and often dangerous work of hunting — and it was not for sport, but in grim earnest, with starvation often the penalty if the hunter failed. Killing a deer with a high-powered rifle and bringing it home on the fender of a car is one thing; killing it with a stone-headed arrow and carrying it ten miles on your back to camp is quite another. Men also made weapons, snowshoes, and canoes, built palisades and lodges, and did the hard work of

canoeing and portaging. In a word, they did what was beyond the strength of women to do.

In hunting and warfare the Indian developed that almost uncanny skill in trailing, observation and deduction of the signs about him, knowledge of the habits of animals, and how to use materials at hand for livelihood, sometimes called "woodcraft." By these pursuits, also, he kept himself in hard and athletic condition.

When food was plenty, the Indians feasted and were merry. They were great gamblers, enjoyed visiting, dancing, and singing. Some of them were fine storytellers; they liked jokes and had a strong sense of humor, and their mythology was often elaborate and even beautiful. Yet hardship was part of their daily life. Sometimes famine came, and they died of starvation by scores. Pestilences swept them away. And they lived in constant peril: from wild beasts; from the elements, especially in the wintry north; and above all from enemies.

This brings us to one of the dominant traits of the savage Indians, and one of the reasons for the small population, for at Columbus' first arrival there were no more than 850,000, and perhaps as few as 350,-

000, of them, in the present area of the United States.

Most tribes were warlike. They did not live in peace before the white man came. Almost constantly they raided and fought against each other; and it is only fair to say that the ferocious bloodlust of some tribes was to blame for white wars against them, just as the white man's greed for land caused many Indian attacks on him.

Indians fought for revenge, hereditary hatred, glory, or simply for love of fighting. War was the chief, almost the only way for an Indian to win distinction. Some tribes dedicated themselves to war as their major aim. For example, before the white man ever came into contact with them, the Iroquois were engaged in destroying the tribes about them. That ferocious confederation of warriors *within historic times* wiped out a score or more of lesser tribes, a total of between 75,000 and 100,000 people. Of the Iroquois, Francis Parkman, the great historian, wrote: "But for the presence of Europeans [they] would probably have subjugated, absorbed, or exterminated every other Indian community east of the Mississippi and north of the Ohio."

Indians carried on warfare mercilessly, killing

women and children of hostile tribes, as well as the men, and expecting the same from their enemies. Some tribes scalped fallen foes, though the custom was by no means universal, nor was it confined to the Indians. At first scalping was practiced only by the woodland Indians of the east, and its general spread was caused partly by "scalp bounties" offered by

colonial and other governments during various frontier wars. White frontiersmen sometimes scalped enemies as freely as did the Indians.

Cruelty was common among Indians, and to show pity was often considered weakness. Frequently — though not always — war prisoners were tortured to death. Yet the red man had no copyright on cruelty. In supposedly civilized Europe more persons died by fire for religious differences, or superstitious charges of witchcraft, or various crimes than were burned to death in all the Indian wars put together.

Among savage Indians, indeed, torture sometimes was a sort of honor, an opportunity for a foe to show his fortitude. And strangely enough, the ordeal was almost willingly accepted by very brave Indian warriors in the hands of their enemies.

Parkman tells of an Iroquois, captured by the Hurons, who was addressed almost affectionately, in this manner:

"My nephew, take courage, and prepare to die tonight like a brave man."

The prisoner coolly asked what would be the manner of his death.

"By fire," was the reply.

"It is well," returned the Iroquois.

He was given a farewell feast, a pipe to smoke, and at the end of this he said, "My brothers, I am about to die. Do your worst to me. I do not fear torture or death."

Nor did he; and under the terrible torments that followed, he was constantly flattered and complimented for his bravery, until he died.

Hatreds that sprang from such wars were deep-bitten, and often worked in the interest of the white man. Almost always the white invaders were able to use one tribe against another. Only in rare instances was there any sort of unity among the tribes against the common enemy — and it was always of short duration.

Yet the Indian had many noble qualities. He was brave, enduring, and loyal to his people and his friends. He was athletic and very shrewd in his own fields of knowledge. He had a natural gift of moving and eloquent speech, and in our history are records of powerful native utterances, such as the speeches of Cornplanter, Red Jacket, Logan, Pontiac, Tecumseh, Joseph of the Nez Percés, and many others. Sometimes, it is true, the Indian was treacherous; but he had a liberal education in treachery from the white man.

We shall not, in this book, discuss voyages or expeditions of exploration, such as those of the Spaniards in the south and southwest. The Indian wars of this country properly begin with the first permanent settlements of white men on its coasts.

In almost three centuries of warfare the white man almost always had the superior weapons, the better organization, the greater resources. But he did not excel his red foe in courage. And with all his disadvantages, the Indian warrior resisted so stubbornly, and often so heroically — even when faced by sheer despair — that he won the reluctant yet genuine respect of his white adversary, which continues to this day.

White man's flint

Red man's flint

The First Great Foe of the White Man | 2

For more than thirty miles, from Point Comfort to Henrico's Hundred, just below the falls of the James River, the English colonists of the infant settlement of Jamestown had cleared away the forests and placed in cultivation most of the broad tongue of land which lay between the James and York Rivers of Virginia.

In the fifteen years since 1607, when the first colonists landed, there had been great setbacks, but now it appeared that prosperity at last had come, and the eighty plantations with their small homes, scattered up and down the two rivers, wore an air of leisurely, peaceful comfort. Men worked in the fields with hoe, plow, or axe. Women and children went about their doings happily and with no dream of danger.

Yet on that morning of March 22, 1622, an appalling horror hung over the entire colony.

In the edges of the forest which surrounded the open fields, crouched dark figures — Indian warriors, painted and armed. They were of all the tribes making up the Powhatan confederacy of Virginia — the flower of scores of villages, eager youths, braves in their prime, stern, responsible chiefs. All were as tense for war as a bowstring drawn to its limit and ready to loose.

Among those warriors in the pride of their vigor walked an old man — a terrible old man. He was seventy-seven years old; his hair was streaked with gray, and he no longer had the strength of the weapon-wielding arm or the fleetness of foot on the path which once he had known. But he had something else: a steady, burning, unchanging hatred, ability to watch while others slept, the cunning of a wolf, and the patience of a spider awaiting the exact moment to spring on the prey in its web. Wherever he went, all men turned to him, for he was held in almost superstitious awe and respect by his people. He was Opechancanough, the great head chief whose name was a legend. And this was the day when his long-matured plans were at last to bear fruit — bloody fruit.

Gazing out from his covert on the white men in their fields, Opechancanough could remember when the first of them came in their three ships fifteen years before: the building of their cabins of logs, and the ensuing troubles. He could remember, and with a red fire of rage, that bewhiskered chief of the white men — him they called Captain John Smith.

Theirs had been a personal feud — Opechancanough's and Smith's. First Opechancanough captured the captain, after killing his two men, and carried him, wounded, to the village of his brother, Powhatan (where today stands the city of Richmond), to be put to death. But Powhatan spared the bearded prisoner at the pleadings of his young daughter, Pocahontas, who later married the white man John Rolfe and was taken across the sea, where she died of smallpox.

It was Smith who captured Opechancanough the

second time. The white chief strode into the Indian's lodge with a band of men, pointed a pistol at him, and marched him to Jamestown under threat of instant death if any of his warriors interfered. There the white men held him prisoner until the Indians brought many canoe loads of corn to buy his freedom.

For the Indians it would have been well if Pow-

hatan had killed Captain Smith in the first instance; and it would have been well for the English had Smith killed Opechancanough in the second — because the chief never forgot the shame of it.

Yet Opechancanough's hatred was more than personal. Powhatan had forbidden an attack that might have destroyed the colony in its early years, saying, "They are only using a little waste land."

But where the Englishman set his hand, he never released what he grasped. Opechancanough had seen the "little waste land" become greater and broader, villages of his own people forced to move to make room for tobacco fields, the forest cut back more and more, and the game driven away by the white man's noise. Other grievances piled up: Indians had been murdered; they had been cheated in trades; drunkenness was fostered among them by white men, because a drunken Indian was easy to defraud; some even had been enslaved to work in the fields.

These things had festered in Opechancanough's mind, but not until Powhatan's death in 1618 could he do anything about them. Even then it took time before he could convince the tribes that he was fitter to lead than his lazy, pleasure-loving elder brother, Opitchapan. So it was not until he was almost seventy-five years old that Opechancanough became chief.

During the two years since then, he had devoted himself to his great plan — the destruction of all the white men's settlements in his country. That he had brought his plan to the present moment without one hint of it reaching the English — though it meant countless councils and endless plotting — is proof of the respect his people had for his commands. Now at last had come the moment.

What exactly was the signal, we do not know, for no white person survived to tell of it. But whether it was a shot, or the waving of a blanket, or the beat of a drum, at eight o'clock that fateful morning of March 22, 1622, from their hiding places all about the unsuspecting plantations, Opechancanough's warriors burst in a tempest of wrath.

It fell upon the settlers like a lightning stroke. Yelling Indians shot down men in the fields, tomahawked women and their babes in their homes, set fire to houses, and carried off anything — weapons, clothing, utensils, or otherwise — that took their savage fancy.

Within a brief time, some say only one hour, 347 men, women, and children were butchered. None whom the Indians reached were spared. In that time all but six of the eighty plantations were destroyed.

The six that were saved were close to Jamestown. Even they, and probably the town itself, would have fallen to the merciless savages, but for the warning

of one Christian Indian. This man, whose name was Chanco, learned of the plot at the last minute, and reached Jamestown just in time to bring word of it. The palisades were manned, and messengers sent out, but only six plantations were reached in time.

Driven back from the fortified town, and forced to be content with the success they had already gained, Opechancanough's warriors slipped back into their forests. The chief was furious at the last-minute failure that deprived him of his final, most desired prey — Jamestown and its people. He could do nothing more, and so disappeared with the rest.

Now, however, came the reckoning.

Within Jamestown, as the full extent of the horror was learned, the stout English hearts only beat the stronger with wrath. Every man who could handle a gun was mustered. In companies they marched forth, leaving behind only enough to guard the palisades.

As they advanced up the neck of land, their anger grew fiercer at the sight of the bloody havoc. They found bodies of their friends, worried and mutilated as if by wild animals, and these they buried. No Indians were seen, and having done all they could, the companies returned to the town.

Sir Francis Wyatt, the governor, called his leading men together, and in a bitter council they declared a war to the finish. Companies were to visit every village within marching distance, burn it, and destroy the crops of corn. Furthermore, these visits were to be repeated thrice each year, to prevent the savages from replanting their crops, or rebuilding their villages. Every Indian found was to be killed on sight.

Meantime, Opechancanough strove to keep his

scattered tribesmen under his control. They showed, however, the usual tendency of savages, and, wearying of discipline, retreated farther into the forest. The old chief was far from cowed. By sheer force of personality he gathered a large number of warriors at Pamunkey, a village where the Pamunkey and Mattapony Rivers join, and there he bravely met Governor Wyatt's small army in a pitched battle.

English muskets were too much for Indian arrows. In the smoke and leaden hail, Opechancanough's warriors broke and fled in a disastrous rout. The village, which had housed 1000 Indians, was destroyed. Opechancanough himself was reported killed, and the colony breathed more freely.

Yet for fourteen years the war continued, until both sides were exhausted. By a treacherous promise of peace, one of the Indian tribes was lured back to its former village. White musketeers surrounded it by night, and next morning massacred every soul in it. That seemed to be the final blow. By 1638 the Indians were so broken and in flight that Jamestown believed peace at last had come.

It was a false dream. Fierce old Opechancanough was not dead. He had escaped to the interior, where he had hidden through all those years, still bitter in his hatred, still scheming to destroy the white men in his land.

Twenty-two years after his first great massacre — in 1644 — his second plan matured. The aged chief was now ninety-nine years old, by far the oldest of any of the great Indian foes who have confronted the white man. Too feeble to walk any distance, he traveled from place to place in a litter, carried by his faithful warriors.

Yet his mind was as keen as ever, and it is proof of his great force of personality that, ancient as he was, scarcely able to stand erect, and almost sightless, he still kept the confidence of his desperate people.

Again the utmost secrecy prevailed — secrecy almost unbelievable since so many knew his plan. A whole new generation of warriors served Opechancanough by this time. He had outlived their fathers, but they still gave him their loyalty.

The aged chief chose April 18, 1644, for his great attack. Early that morning his braves burst as before upon the settlements, killing with relentless fury. In a single day between 350 and 500 colonists were slaughtered.

But Virginia had grown greatly in population, and the governor, Sir William Berkeley, was a man of decision. Hastily gathering a force, he marched at once and drove back the Indians.

Once more the relentless counterattack began. The hostile tribesmen were hunted down, killed, or enslaved. And at last old Opechancanough himself was captured. He was carried on a stretcher to Jamestown, to be exhibited in triumph. There a soldier, perhaps half crazed by loss of friends or relatives in the massacre, deliberately shot and fatally wounded him.

Governor Berkeley himself went to see the dying chief. The old man, who had seen nearly a century pass in his lifetime, gathered his last strength and spoke to the governor. His words were interpreted as follows: "Had it been my fortune to take Sir William Berkeley prisoner, I would not have meanly exposed him as a show to my people."

A few minutes later he died.

After his death Virginia had other Indian troubles, but never again would the colony be threatened with complete destruction. And be this remembered: had it not been for one small slip in Opechancanough's plans on that fatal March day in 1622 — the defection of Chanco, who preferred his Christian faith to his own blood — Jamestown as a colony might have shared the fate of that earlier sister colony on Roanoke Island which utterly disappeared, the details of its doom not known to this day.

Opechancanough was the first great Indian chief to oppose the white man with deadly and lifelong enmity. He had his faults — vanity, vindictiveness, and cruelty among them. But he was, according to his own lights, a patriot: the first to grasp the dire meaning to his people of the spread of the white men over the land.

There would be others, beginning soon, who would continue the long fight he had been the first to launch.

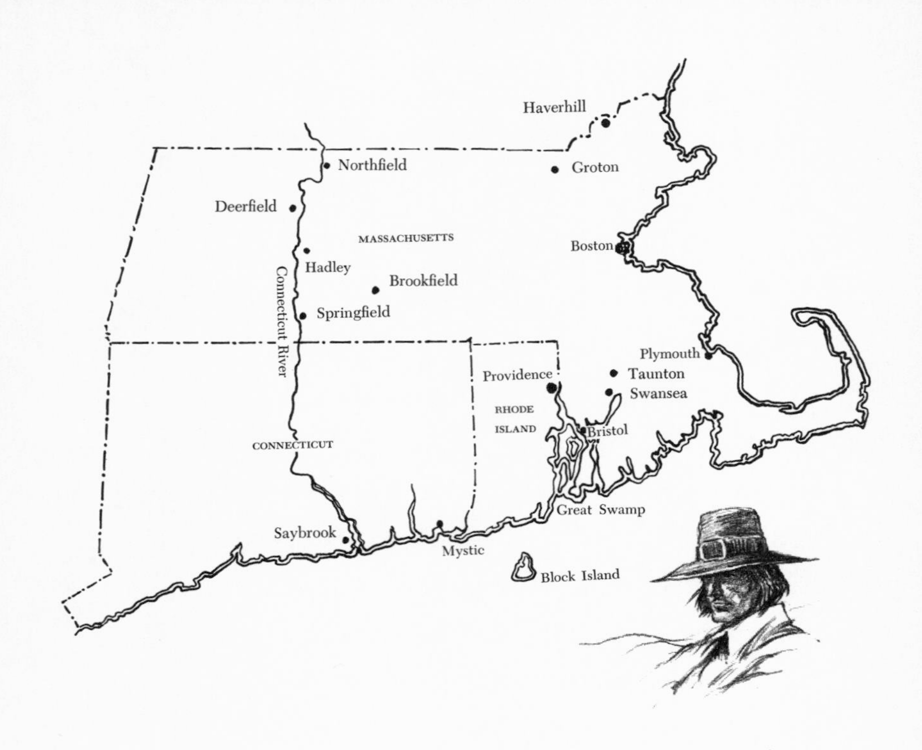

The Puritans and King Philip | 3

A NEAT LITTLE FISHING SMACK was bobbing over the waves in a crisp breeze off Block Island, south of Rhode Island, on a summer day in 1636. Her captain and owner was John Gallup, of Boston Town. As crew he had a man and two boys, with nets and fishlines, for already thus early fisheries were important in New England. As the smack came around a point of land, Gallup saw another ship. He probably recognized it: a craft somewhat larger than his own, belonging to John Oldham, an Indian trader, and one of the founders of the new Connecticut colony.

"There's something wrong with that ship!" Gallup exclaimed.

She was drifting with sails flapping, showing that no one was at the tiller, although a number of figures were moving about on her deck. Then suddenly a canoe filled with Indians shoved off on the other side, and paddled hastily for the island shore.

It burst upon Gallup that the vessel had been overwhelmed by savages, the entire crew probably murdered.

"Hard at her!" he cried to the helmsman.

As the smack bore down on the other craft, Gallup saw some Indians still on the deck, and opened fire on them, using two muskets, which the boys kept loading for him. One Indian after another fell, and then several leaped overboard and swam for the shore.

A moment later Gallup's brave little craft struck the side of the other ship with a crash that heeled it well over. Followed by his small crew, the Boston fisherman leaped to the deck of the Oldham vessel. Only four Indians remained on it, and they were at once made prisoners.

The ship was a shambles, its crew and master murdered and scalped. Indians from Block Island — Pequots — had come aboard pretending to trade, then had fallen upon and slain all the white men. They were in the act of plundering the craft when Gallup arrived.

Before a magistrate the prisoners not only confessed to the attack on Oldham's ship, but added that another trading vessel, belonging to a Captain Stone, had also been captured and the crew murdered. These acts, they said, were in revenge. The Stone

ship had enticed aboard one of their chiefs, seized and bound him, and demanded of his people a bushel of wampum — native shell beads that passed as money — for ransom. When the price was paid, the chief was returned to them, dead.

The Pequots were a tribe whose name (from the word *Paquataug,* meaning "Destroyers") showed their fierce and warlike nature. The rapid spread of white settlements up and down the shores of New England since the first landing of the Pilgrims in

1620 had caused among these Indians growing unrest. It came to a head with Captain Stone's treacherous act.

War began very soon after, in that summer of 1636. The Indians struck first, killing a few white settlers and burning some cabins. Then the English came to the Pequot country, in a campaign short and brutal.

Led by Captain John Mason, a veteran soldier, a force of 100 stern musketeers and 150 Mohegan warriors, under their famous chief Uncas, who was ever a steadfast friend to the white man, surprised a Pequot village at what is now Mystic, Connecticut.

A charge at dawn by the soldiers, and the tinder-dry bark wigwams were set blazing by brands thrown among them. What followed was ghastly. In a few minutes the village was a roaring inferno of flames, and the soldiers and Mohegans simply shot down or tomahawked those who tried to escape. No Indian war party was ever guilty of a massacre more dreadful. Probably 600 Pequots of all ages and both sexes died wretchedly in the fire, or were otherwise slaughtered. The survivors fled from the country, and save for a few small bands, ceased to exist as a separate people.

But their burning village was like a fiery beacon,

warning other tribes of danger, calling on them for revenge.

Before the snow was melted in the spring of 1675, some men made a shocking discovery — the body of a dead man was under the ice of Assawompsett Pond, near what is now Middleboro, Massachusetts. When it was taken out, the body was identified as that of Sassamon, a "Praying Indian," that is, one who was Christianized.

Shortly after, three members of the Wampanoag tribe were arrested, convicted, and two hanged, while the other was shot, for the murder. But the colonists had deeper suspicions. They believed the murder had been instigated by Philip, Chief of the Wampanoags. There was reason for these suspicions. Sassamon, who could read and write, had served for a time as secretary to the chief, and then, acting the part of a spy and informer, carried to the Governor of Plymouth word that Philip was making a great plot against the white men. The chief could hardly be blamed for ordering the renegade's death.

Nevertheless, the death of Sassamon was the first act in what was to be known in history as King Philip's War.

The Wampanoags, living in southern Massachusetts, had a long record of friendship toward the English. Their great chief Massassoit had protected and even fed the early Plymouth colonists.

But Massassoit had died in 1661, and things changed. He had two sons, Wamsutta, whom the English called Alexander, and Metacom, known as Philip and later as King Philip.

Alexander, who became Chief at his father's death, lived only a few months. Suspected by the colonists of plotting with the Narragansets, he was arrested and taken to Plymouth. Not long afterward, he

King Philip

died: of "excessive rage and mortification," according to the English; of poison, according to the Indians.

Philip, who then became Chief, undoubtedly believed his older brother had been murdered. It was only one of many grievances to whet his rage at seeing his people displaced, driven out, victimized, and despised by the ever-spreading white settlers.

Yet he concealed his hatred, even signing a treaty of friendship — of which he probably did not understand the context — while he engaged in intense activity, studying his enemy, making plans, and winning other tribes to his cause. For nine years he continued, traveling as far north as Maine to enlist the support of the fierce Abnakis, persuading the tribes of Connecticut, Massachusetts, and Rhode Island to join him, and even winning over many of the "Praying Indians," who lived in separate villages from their pagan brethren.

Sassamon's death interrupted these careful plans before they were finished. But Philip knew the time had come, and retired with his people to his chief village, Pokanoket, on Bristol peninsula, near the present city of Bristol, Rhode Island.

For a time there was an uneasy truce. Then an Indian was killed by a white man near Swansea, a hamlet less than ten miles from Pokanoket, and everyone knew the act might bring on hostilities.

Sunday, June 24, 1675, was appointed a day of fasting and prayer that the horrors of Indian warfare might be averted. It was that very Sunday which Philip chose for his first blow, and it was at Swansea that he directed it. Services were just over, and the people were returning to their homes, when gunfire was heard — the Wampanoags were shooting down the churchgoers!

In that first flurry of killing, nine persons died and two were wounded. When the survivors fled next day to Providence for refuge, Swansea was burned to the ground. It is noteworthy that Philip gave an order to spare the four colonists and their families who had done him kindnesses — James Brown, Captain Thomas Willett, James Leonard, and Hugh Cole. These departed in safety.

But war at last had come. In New England villages drums rattled and armed men mustered to defend their homes. And here came welcome help: in spite of Philip's blandishments, Uncas and his Mohegans remained faithful to the white men. With

150 of his warriors the chief fought well in the following campaigns. The addition of the forest-wise Mohegans was most fortunate, for Philip's tactics baffled ordinary military maneuvers.

Wherever possible, he avoided any stand in which the white man's superior discipline and weapons could be brought to bear on his warriors. Like serpents the Indians appeared out of the forest in swift raids, struck, and glided back again. No one knew where next they might come, but everyone knew that when they came death and destruction were sure to follow. All New England was thrown into a panic.

Sometimes the inexperience of the white soldiers caused them to blunder into bloody traps. Late in June a large force of Plymouth and Massachusetts colony men located Philip and some of his warriors in Pocasset Swamp. They surrounded it, believing they had the red leader trapped.

Events soon revealed that the trap was the other way around. A few Wampanoags showed themselves at one side of the swamp. At once the colonists charged — and suddenly found themselves ambushed in a morass. In that bog, with the gloom of early evening making still darker the heavy woods, they lost a number of men and managed to retreat with difficulty.

Having repulsed his white foes, Philip and his braves slipped away in canoes up the nearby Taunton River. Yet at this moment of victory the chief suffered his first setback. Paddling up the stream, the Wampanoags were themselves ambushed — by Uncas and his Mohegans. Several of their warriors were slain before they broke out of the trap and reached central Massachusetts.

By the fall of 1675 disaster seemed to be over-

whelming New England everywhere. The Nipmucks, Pennacooks, and Connecticut River tribes had joined Philip's war, and the Narragansets of Rhode Island, under their chief Canonchet, had taken up the hatchet. From the north the Abnakis descended with tomahawk and scalping knife on the settlements of Maine and New Hampshire. Many Massachusetts towns were devastated or abandoned.

There were hero tales in those times. On Sunday, August 1, while the people of Hadley, on the Connecticut River, were at prayer, the dread war whoop was heard and services ended abruptly. Men carried weapons with them, even to church. Now they seized their guns and formed outside to repel the foe, while the women and children huddled within for safety.

On came the Indians, yelling and firing, burning outlying buildings, and in such numbers that it is small wonder that the few settlers began to waver and show signs of flight.

At this moment a strange figure suddenly appeared as if from nowhere: a tall old man with white hair and beard, grim-faced and fiery-eyed, with a sword in hand. From his manner of handling the sword and his way of giving orders it was clear that he was accustomed to war and knew how to command. The colonists rallied. When he led a charge, they followed him and drove off the Indians.

And then, when they turned to thank their deliverer, he was gone! As unaccountably as he had come, he disappeared.

Many of the people of Hadley believed he was a messenger from heaven sent to save them. But in later years his identity was learned. He was General William Goffe, who had been a commander under Cromwell, and was one of the judges who condemned King Charles I to death. When Cromwell died and Charles II came to the throne, the "regicides" — king killers, of whom Goffe was one — were hunted down, and hanged or imprisoned for life. A few escaped and fled to other countries, Goffe making his way to Massachusetts and hiding in the home of a friend named Russell in Hadley, where he returned after the battle. At the time of the fight he was seventy years old. He died peacefully in 1679, four years later.

Not so glorious were other encounters. Captain Beers, with 30 men, marching to relieve Northfield, was ambushed at Sawmill Brook, September 3, and died with 20 of his men. A force of 90 soldiers under Captain Lathrop halted to rest by a little stream not far from Deerfield, and scattered about, gathering wild grapes. Suddenly a horde of Nipmucks, who had followed them all night, burst upon them. In the bloody action that followed, 83 colonists, including Lathrop, were killed, only seven escaping.

Hearing the firing, Captain Moseley hurried to the rescue with a few men from Deerfield, only to find the Indians turning to attack him. He would have shared Lathrop's fate but for the lucky arrival of a third force under Robert Treat which repulsed the savages and saved the survivors. The waters of the little stream over which this series of fights took place ran red that day, and ever since it has been known as Bloody Brook.

In that terrible summer Middleboro, Brookfield, Deerfield, Northfield, Dartmouth, Providence, Rehe-both, Taunton, Sudbury, Hingham, Weymouth, Groton, Braintree, Northampton, Springfield, Westfield, and many lesser places all knew the torch and tomahawk. Western Massachusetts, New Hampshire, and Maine were practically swept bare of white settlers.

But in December the colonists struck back. The Narragansets had fortified themselves with a strong palisade in a winter camp in the Great Swamp of southeastern Rhode Island. There, on Sunday, December 19, a force of 979 men from the Massachusetts, Plymouth, and Connecticut colonies, together with Uncas and his braves, attacked this stronghold.

It was cold, with deep snow, and the swamp was frozen. With wild yells the Indians opened fire on their enemies. A charge by the Massachusetts company at the single gate was driven back with heavy

loss. For a time the battle raged furiously on that wintry day, neither side advancing or retreating, white men and red falling where they stood.

In the colonial force was Captain Benjamin Church of Duxbury, who had spent enough time among the Indians so that he alone of the commanders seemed able to match their stratagems. While the fight raged in front of the stockade, Church led his Plymouth men around through the frozen swamp to the rear, where he ordered them to pry apart the logs of the palisade.

Very quickly the Narragansets came shooting. Wounded three times, Church led his men through the breach they had made. The enemy warriors charged him so fiercely that it was a question whether he and his men could escape being killed inside the palisade where they had entered.

At this crisis, Church ordered the torch put to the bark wigwams, as had Mason before him at the Pequot fort. And now the dreadful scene of that former massacre was re-enacted. With their village in flames and the white men and Mohegans surrounding them, the Narragansets thought only of escape. Some, their chief Canonchet among them, got away, but hundreds died by bullet or tomahawk, or the flames of their burning dwellings. The colonists lost 6 captains and 120 men.

It was the bloodiest battle, and perhaps the decisive one, of the war. Yet though this victory broke the power of the Narragansets, the year 1676 opened badly for the colonies. Lancaster was destroyed by the Indians, while Plymouth, Providence, and even Boston were threatened.

In March came a defeat with a grimly humorous aspect. Canonchet had retreated with the remnant of his Narraganset warriors to the head of Narragansett Bay. There Captain Pierce (or Pierse) attacked him with 60 Plymouth men.

The Indians fought desperately and drove the colonists back. Hurriedly, Pierce sent a messenger galloping to Providence, five miles south, begging Captain Edmunds for reinforcements.

But when the messenger arrived, Edmunds was in church. It was not good etiquette to interrupt an important Puritan at worship, so the messenger, with more consideration than good sense, waited until the last "Amen" was said, the last hymn sung, before he presented his message.

By then it was too late. Though Edmunds gath-

ered a force and hurried to the battle scene, the Indians were gone. Of Pierce's 60 men, 52 lay dead.

That was Canonchet's last victory. He was surprised and captured on April 3 and taken to Stonington, Connecticut, where his captors offered him his life if his Narragansets would surrender. He would not even discuss it. When he heard the sentence of death he said, "I like it well. I shall die before my heart is soft, or I have said anything unworthy of myself." A firing squad of three Indian allies of the white men executed him.

With his greatest ally gone, Philip knew he was fighting a losing war. And on his trail like a bloodhound was his most able enemy, Benjamin Church, with a picked band of frontiersmen and Mohegans. Relentlessly the captain pursued the Wampanoag chief, wherever report said he was, never ceasing and using every Indian trick and wile in the long hunt until Philip was dead.

Connecticut at this time offered the first of the notorious "scalp bounties" which became a disgrace to civilized white man. For each hostile warrior's scalp the price was "A coat, that is, two yards of trucking [trade] cloth, worth five shillings per yard; and for every one brought in alive, two coats; for King Philip's head, twenty coats, and if taken alive, forty coats."

With his warriors falling away from him, Philip, like a hunted animal, sought refuge in his home forests near Mount Hope on the Bristol peninsula. He knew the country, and hoped perhaps once more to throw his enemies off his trail.

Church, with his picked company, was grimly on the track. Philip's wife and young son were captured, and promptly sold as slaves. On the night of August 11, Church found the chief's camp in a swamp near the foot of Mount Hope. He placed his men about it. Next morning, August 12, a single Indian was seen coming, and one of the red allies recognized him.

"That is Philip — shoot!" he cried.

A colonist pressed his trigger but his musket failed to fire. Then the Indian, who was called Alderman, raised his gun and aimed. Evidently the weapon was loaded with buckshot. At its report, Philip fell forward on his face in the mud and water of the swamp, his musket beneath him. One shot had passed through his heart, another not two inches from it. He was beheaded and his head taken by his slayer for the reward.

Philip's death was the real end of the war, though depredations continued for some time, and not until April, 1678, was a treaty signed at Casco, Maine (which then was part of the Massachusetts colony). With that treaty the tribes buried the hatchet and exchanged prisoners with the whites.

It had been a costly war. Sixteen towns in Massachusetts and four in Rhode Island were utterly destroyed, besides many that were severely damaged. No colonist was left alive in Maine, and New Hampshire was almost as nearly swept bare.

More than 500 buildings were burned, and at least 600 white lives lost, not counting scores carried into captivity.

But the Indians were crushed. Most of them fled, some as far as the Illinois country.

And Philip? "A doleful great naked dirty beast," Benjamin Church remembered him from having looked on him in death. He had had reason to be doleful. He had chosen the wrong time. A generation earlier he might have wiped out the English, but the stubborn colonists were too much for him when at last he took to the warpath.

Yet he left seeds of further wars behind him. The English colonists were bitterly to learn, from the Abnakis and other tribes in the future, that Philip's hatred lingered on after his death.

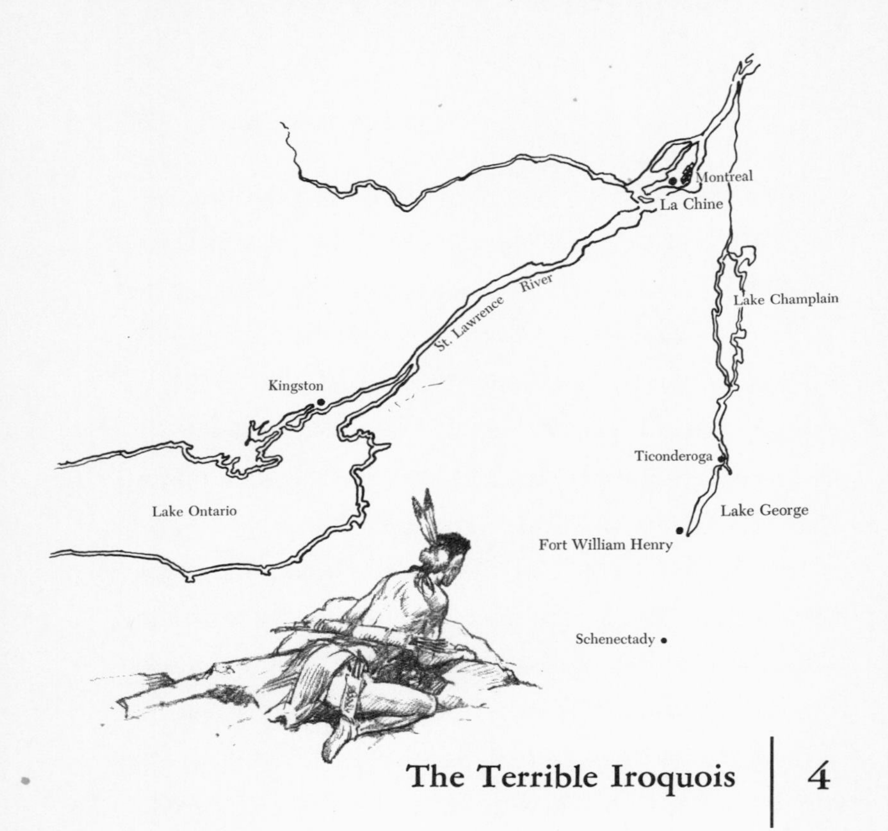

The Terrible Iroquois | 4

In dealing with Indians, the French were infinitely superior to the English. For one thing, they cared little for land and devoted themselves to the fur trade; the English were intent on carving out for themselves farms and building homes and cities in the New World. For another, the French adapted themselves easily to Indian customs, often married into Indian tribes, and treated the Indians as friends and equals; the English disliked and distrusted the red men.

As a result, the French ranged the continent — La Salle down the Ohio and Mississippi Rivers, Radisson north to Hudson's Bay, Vérendrye west as far as the Rocky Mountains and Wyoming, to mention only a few; the English long were held to the Atlantic Coast. Yet almost at the beginning of their relations with the Indians, the French made their one great and fatal mistake.

On July 3, 1608, Samuel de Champlain, the "Father of Canada," founded the first French settlement at Quebec, and soon made an alliance with the neighboring Indian tribes. He had no idea of the gravity of the step he was taking. Those Indians happened to be Hurons and Algonkins, mortal enemies of the Iroquois, and by binding himself to them, Champlain committed France to a feud that in the end would do much to ruin her hopes in America.

The following year, 1609, Champlain and two Frenchmen accompanied a party of Hurons up the Richelieu River, and discovered the beautiful lake that bears his name. On July 29, near the present site of Ticonderoga, a band of hostile Indians — Iroquois — appeared, and gave battle. The Frenchmen opened fire on the enemy with their arquebuses (very primitive muskets). Three savages were cut down by their shots, and the smoke and noise of their guns, the first seen and heard in these wilds, so astonished and terrified the hostiles that they scattered and fled.

Champlain won a victory that day, but in a sense he lost a continent. The shot that brought down the first Iroquois brave started a sequence of events from which the French never were able entirely to retreat. Thereafter, like it or not, they were identified usually with the enemies of the Iroquois, and suffered accordingly.

The warrior race thus alienated was in many ways the most remarkable in America. Called the "Five Nations" then, the Iroquois were a league of kindred tribes, living in northern New York and ranging from the Hudson River to the Niagara country in the following order, from east to west: Mohawks, Oneidas, Onondagas, Cayugas, and Senecas. Later (about 1713), by the addition of the Tuscaroras, they became known as the "Six Nations."

They lived in "long houses," dwellings of beams roofed with bark, sometimes 100 feet long and housing several families, in villages surrounded by strong log palisades. These towns were fairly permanent, for the Iroquois cultivated the land quite extensively.

Two native geniuses, Hiawatha, a Mohawk (but not the hero of Longfellow's poem), and Dekawanida, an Onondaga, had formed the Iroquois league about 1570. It was a loose but smooth-working confederation, and one of its avowed purposes was *to make war in order to make peace.*

Although the Iroquois never mustered more than 2500 warriors, they were the deadliest and most feared war power of their race. Among the first of the tribes to obtain guns, from Dutch traders, they extended their conquests until their dominion was acknowledged from the Ottawa River in Ontario to the Tennessee River in the south, and from the Kennebec in Maine to the Illinois River and Lake Michigan. Upon the allies of the French — Hurons, Algonkins, Illinois, and others — they fell with such fury that over the years they almost destroyed them.

Wrote Francis Parkman of the Iroquois:

> They made a solitude and called it peace . . . It was not by their craft, nor by their organization . . . that this handful of savages gained bloody supremacy. They

carried all before them because they were animated throughout, as one man, by the same audacious pride and insatiable rage for conquest . . . and they owed their unity and vigor of action to the homicidal frenzy that urged them all alike.

They and their Indian foes were sufficiently cruel and fierce in their tribal wars, but they seemed to reach an especial peak of ferocity when they became involved in the quarrels of white nations — to which the rivalry of France and England inevitably led. The French stimulated the Abnakis, Hurons, Ottawas, and others to massacre English colonies. The English used the Iroquois for the same purpose against the French. It was an ugly policy, a vicious policy, which made a hell of the border for most of a century.

In 1680 the English colonies lay along the Atlantic Coast, east of the Appalachian Mountains. But the French, besides claiming the St. Lawrence Basin and the Great Lakes area, and all to the north, asserted their right, through exploration, to all of interior America. Their grand strategy became a long effort to outflank the English, coming in on them from the rear to conquer them. That master plan was in the end defeated by the dark and deadly Iroquois guarding the area below the Great Lakes.

Jealousy over the fur trade caused the first fighting. Though there was profound peace between Britain and France, with James II of England and Louis XIV of France on friendliest terms, in the distant wilderness of America, French forces cut off English trading expeditions on the lakes and captured English trading posts on Hudson's Bay in a series of sharp little battles.

Those fights in the far north were like a fuse to a train of giant explosions. The English public, in the colonies and at home, was enraged; and the bad blood grew, even though King James ordered Governor Thomas Dongan of New York to "keep a friendly correspondence" with his rival, and "take good care to give him no cause for complaint."

In the summer of 1680 the Iroquois made a gigantic raid against the French allied tribes camped about Fort St. Louis on the Illinois River. They almost destroyed those villages, slaughtering hundreds, and, as Parkman wrote, "returned with several hundred prisoners, of whom they burned those that were useless, and incorporated the young and strong into their own tribe."

Governor Denonville of Canada resolved to punish them. His first act was to seize, treacherously, 51 *friendly* Iroquois, and ship them to France as galley slaves. (The French used the outmoded galleys, rowed by slaves chained to the oars, as part of their navy in the Mediterranean until as late as 1748.)

Then Denonville mustered at Fort Frontenac (where Kingston, Ontario, now stands), an army of nearly 1000 men — soldiers, Canadian bush rangers, and Indians, chiefly Hurons, Potawatomies, Sauks, Foxes, Chippewas (Ojibwas), and Ottawas.

Young Baron de Lahontan, a junior officer, wrote of these Indian allies:

> Never had Canada seen such a sight. Most of them wore nothing but horns on their heads, and the tails of beasts behind their backs. Their faces were painted red or green, with black or white spots; their ears and noses were hung with ornaments of iron; and their naked bodies were daubed with the figures of various sorts of animals.

Crossing the eastern arm of Lake Ontario with this motley array, Denonville began a slow march through the tangled forest. The Senecas, most westerly of the Five Nations, learned of the invasion and prepared.

On a heated afternoon, July 13, 1687, while the French advance guard of 800 men pushed its way wearily through the marshes and heavy woods, there came a sudden uproar of gunfire, accompanied by blood-chilling war whoops. Men began to fall. A moment later, as painted savages bounded through the trees to tomahawk them, the advance guard went reeling back.

The Senecas, greatly outnumbered, had neatly ambushed Denonville, and for a time they were

near to winning a smashing victory. But the governor and his officers rallied their men, the French regulars and their Indian allies pressed forward, firing grew heavier each minute, and the Senecas were gone as quickly as they came.

They left 27 dead warriors on the field. Denonville's loss was about equal. He did not pursue, having discovered the perils of blind warfare in the tangled forest. When later he moved cautiously forward, he found the Seneca "castle" (fortified town), burned and abandoned. The tribe had gone to their neighbors, the Cayugas, to the east. Denonville could only retreat to Canada.

The invasion infuriated the Iroquois. That winter their war parties ranged through the French settle-

ments like lynxes, keeping forts and settlements in virtual siege and bringing trade and commerce to a standstill.

It was not until the summer of 1689, however, their their real vengeance fell. In the midst of a violent hailstorm, the night of August 4, a great war party of 1500 braves paddled across the St. Lawrence and stole down on the settlement of La Chine, about six miles above Montreal.

Suddenly in the darkness rose the death yell, and the most terrible massacre in Canadian history began. Furious with blood-lust the Iroquois burst into houses, looting, burning, and slaying men, women, and children without mercy.

A terrified refugee managed to reach Montreal, and a detachment of troops marched to La Chine

— too late. They found every house burned and the bodies of the settlers strewn among them, or hanging from stakes where they had been tortured. The soldiers retreated.

Next day a company of 80 men, marching toward Montreal, was cut to pieces by a horde of savages. Only six escaped death and scalping.

Montreal was wild with terror. For weeks the Iroquois hung about, burning every house outside the city's ring of forts, looting, and killing. More than 200 settlers died, and when the Iroquois departed they carried away 120 captives, many to meet death by fire. Their own losses were almost nothing.

While all Canada lay stunned by this disaster, news came that the English people had forced James II to abdicate his throne, placing William, Prince of Orange, and his wife Mary in the seat of power in his stead.

Louis XIV of France backed the cause of James, and France and England declared war. It was the first of four wars in America, each related to a great European war. This one was called by the colonists King William's War, but in Europe it was the War of the Grand Alliance, 1689–97. It was followed by Queen Anne's War (War of the Spanish

Succession, 1702–13), King George's War (War of the Austrian Succession, 1744–48), and the French and Indian War (Seven Years' War, 1756–63).

During all that time there was scarcely a break in hostilities in the American colonies, for raiding, burning, and killing by the Indians went on even in the truces between these "official" conflicts.

Denonville was replaced as Governor of Canada by the Count de Frontenac, a great man and a veteran in administration of French American colonies. He at once struck at the English colonies. Knowing his French were far outnumbered by the English, he fell back on Indian war parties, led by Frenchmen and largely consisting of Hurons, Abnakis, and Iroquois converted to the Catholic faith. These last had been persuaded by the Jesuits to move to Canada. Their pagan tribesmen proclaimed them traitors, and called them Caghnawagas. In the bloody times that followed it was repeatedly seen that the "Christianized" Iroquois and Abnakis were as fiendishly cruel as the so-called heathen Indians.

During the next fearful months, Dover, Salmon Falls, and Bristol in New Hampshire, Pemaquid and York in Maine, Schenectady in New York, and many other settlements in those colonies and Massachusetts were gutted, burned, and their residents murdered or driven north as prisoners by the Indians. Incredible as it seems, even after being warned, these places often were taken by surprise. For example, Schenectady, a Dutch settlement, left its fort gates open, *guarded only by two snowmen* — built by boys as a prank — the night it was captured and its people massacred.

One Indian raiding party penetrated as far south

as Groton, Massachusetts, within a few miles of Boston, and returned safely to Canada, after murdering 105 persons. All told, hundreds of English settlers were killed or transported to miserable captivity in the frigid north.

Yet through all this agonizing period the English settlers did not quail. Grimly they rebuilt their charred homes and towns, plowed again their fields, and fought back bravely, though at first not very successfully.

There were some heroic deeds. In the spring of 1697 a band of Abnakis swooped on the farms in the vicinity of Haverhill, Massachusetts. One of those farms belonged to Thomas Dustin, whose wife Hannah had borne a child only a week before and was resting with her infant, under the care of a neighbor girl, Mary Neff. Dustin took his other seven children with him when he went to work in his field.

Frightful yells brought his heart to his throat, and he saw Indians assail his house, which soon was burning. At first he started to the rescue, but saw it was too late and began to retreat with his children (the youngest only two years old), holding his gun ready and facing the now pursuing foe. Again and again the savages tried to come up to him, but the menacing musket kept them back. He had only one shot, but none of the Indians wanted to be the one who died by it. And so at last he succeeded in shepherding his little flock to safety in a fortified house that was well defended.

Meanwhile the Indians, first brutally killing the poor little infant, herded Hannah Dustin and Mary Neff with others of their neighbors who had been captured. Those who were unable to travel were tomahawked at once. Then the survivors were parceled out among the Indians, who set out in separate bands for their villages far to the north.

Mrs. Dustin, Mary Neff, and a young boy were given to a party of twelve Abnakis, in which were a squaw and her young son. On the way the Indians terrified their captives with stories of the tortures they would suffer when their destination was reached. But Mrs. Dustin, as brave as any man, made a desperate plan to escape. She whispered it to Mary Neff and the boy, who agreed to help her.

Halfway along their journey the chance came. That night the savages feasted, and feeling safe now from pursuit they all went to sleep. In the still darkness the prisoners stirred, rose silently, took up tomahawks, and crouched, each at the head of a warrior. It was a moment of supreme tension — they must miss no blows, they must kill all the men, or their own fate would be too terrible to think about.

Mrs. Dustin gave the signal. All together they struck, and struck again and again about them, their arms steeled by fear and hate, with blows so rapid and deadly that the ten warriors died almost before they roused from slumber. The squaw, bleeding, ran screeching into the forest with her child.

Throughout the rest of that night the three white prisoners hid, shivering at the thought that other Indians might come. But the great war party had scattered. At dawn Hannah Dustin scalped the ten dead warriors, and led the way home. They found a canoe on the bank of the Merrimack River and, using it, reached the Massachusetts settlements.

She was, of course, overjoyed to find her husband and seven children safe. With the scalps to prove their exploit, the three escaped prisoners were rewarded with many gifts by the colonial government and citizens. But their escape itself was surely the most precious gift of all.

King William's War dragged on. The English home government did little to help the colonies. When the Treaty of Ryswick ended the war in Europe in 1697, it really settled nothing in the American colonies.

There was, however, one important result. The Iroquois and the Maine Indians — notably the Abnakis — agreed to remain neutral henceforth as between the French and English. This proved a great disadvantage for New England and New York, because in Queen Anne's War, which followed in 1702, the Iroquois kept their neutrality promise, while their enemies, and hence those of the English, did not.

All of northern New England was burned and wracked and blackened. Hardly a hamlet in that area escaped. Fine old towns like Groton, Lancaster, Exeter, Dover, Kittery, Casco, Kingston, York, Berwick, Wells, Winter Harbor, Amesbury, Marlborough, and others have dread chapters in their histories telling of the visits of the stealthy and murderous enemy. In a single month, August, 1703, 160 persons were killed or carried off in Maine and New Hampshire.

Most famous of those massacres was that of Deerfield, Massachusetts, on February 29, 1704—a "leap-year day," incidentally. The winter had been cold, so severe, indeed, that though there had been warnings the people could not believe Indians would come from a place as remote as Canada.

Yet that February 50 Canadians and 200 Abnakis and Caghnawagas stealthily filed on snowshoes nearly 300 miles to the settlements without being seen. Their leader was Hertel de Rouville. By the time they reached Deerfield they had used up their

provisions and were wild and fierce with hunger.

Snow lay deep on the ground, drifted up against the walls of the houses scattered along the road toward Hatfield, and against the eight-foot wooden palisade which surrounded the center of town. That night the raiders lay hidden in the woods while one by one the lights of the village went out and families went to sleep. About two hours before dawn, leaving packs and snowshoes behind, they stole toward the doomed town. A crust had frozen on the snow, so hard that Indians and Canadians could mount the drifts to the top of the palisade, and drop silently over inside the enclosure.

Then the hideous sound of war whoops, at the top of savage lungs, awoke Deerfield to the horror that followed. With hatchets or log battering rams the Indians smashed doors and window shutters, then leaped like beasts of prey into the houses, to drag victims from their beds and tomahawk them or drive them out into the bitter night as captives.

In the darkness great bonfires sprang up — homes set in flames — with the skulking, crested figures of Indians outlined now and then in the glare. Shots, screams of victims, and the exultant yells of the savages made a hideous uproar in the night.

The inmates of some houses fought. One house, owned by Captain Sheldon, was taken only when the Indians chopped a hole through the oak door with their hatchets and began shooting those within. That door of "the Old Indian House" is today a prized exhibit in the Deerfield historical museum.

Sergeant Benoni Stebbins and Captain Jonathan Wells also fought back in their homes. Particularly fierce was the attack on the Stebbins house. Inside were Stebbins, David Hoyt, Joseph Catlin, and Benjamin Church (named for the old hero), with three other men, and some of their families. All told there were seven men, four or five women, and a number of children.

Women loaded guns for their husbands, and Hoyt's wife was wounded in the battle. Stebbins was killed and Church wounded, but though the Indians charged repeatedly and tried to set the house on fire, each attack was repelled, and the bodies of the painted foes, sprawled on the bloody snow, showed the price in lives the defenders exacted.

Meantime the alarm reached the nearby towns of Hatfield, Hadley, and Northampton, and armed men began hurrying toward Deerfield. Their rally-

ing point was the Wells house, and with Captain Wells himself at their head, they began to pursue the war party, which drew off, cheated of capturing the Stebbins house but bearing away many prisoners.

A short distance from the town there was a brisk little fight with the enemy rear guard in which both sides lost several men, but the invaders were too strong and the rescuers were beaten off.

Fifty-three were killed in Deerfield, while the war party had 60 dead and many wounded. They carried off, however, 111 prisoners, including the Reverend John Williams, pastor of the village, his wife, and five of their children.

Hardly half of the captives ever reached Canada. In the dreadful march through the frozen forests, Rouville hurried them forward at a pace many of the miserable prisoners could not maintain. These died, or were killed, and among them was Mrs. Eunice Williams, wife of the minister.

Later, after the war, some of the captives, including Reverend Williams, were exchanged for French prisoners. But many never again saw their homes. One was little Eunice Williams, aged seven, the pastor's daughter. She was kept by the Caghnawagas, grew up among them, and became the wife of an Indian, by whom she had several children.

The agony of Deerfield was that of other towns. Except that the English were ceded Acadia (Nova Scotia), which they had captured, nothing was accomplished by the Treaty of Utrecht, signed in 1713, ending Queen Anne's War. And King George's War, which followed in 1744, was really no more than a preliminary to the savage and decisive French and Indian War beginning not long after. It was in this war that one of the world's towering figures, George Washington, made his first appearance in history.

Young Washington and General Braddock | 5

THE ISSUE between Britain and France was too intense to continue long without an explosion of some kind. Each side had certain advantages and disadvantages in the life-and-death struggle that was building up. Along the Atlantic seaboard, the thirteen English colonies by 1750 had a population of perhaps 2,000,000; while in Canada and Louisiana there were only about 80,000 Frenchmen, widely scattered. On the other hand, the English colonies were under separate governments, with so many jealousies and rivalries that they never acted as a unit; the French were under the single head of an absolute dictator — the King of France — moving and acting on orders without question or hesitation. While the English argued and let time pass, the French prepared.

Imagine a gigantic scythe blade, more than 2000 miles long, sweeping from the Gulf of St. Lawrence, up that river, across the lower Great Lakes, then curving down the Mississippi to its delta. That was the formation of the French fortifications: Louisbourg on Cape Breton commanding the mouth of the St. Lawrence River; Quebec, Three Rivers, and Montreal on that great waterway itself; Frontenac, Toronto, and Niagara on Lake Ontario; Presque Isle on one end of Lake Erie and Detroit on the Detroit River guarding the other end; Miami and St. Joseph covering the line to the lower tip of Lake Michigan; and from there, hooking southward in a great sweep along the Mississippi Valley, Vincennes, Cahokia, Chartres, Massaic, Arkansas Post, St. Pierre, Rosalie (Natchez), Baton Rouge, and finally New Orleans.

Behind these crouched still other forts, the whole great system designed both as defensive and offensive points for the coming struggle. As usual, the

French counted on their fierce Indian allies to make up for their own disadvantage in numbers.

The first shot in the inevitable conflict, which was called in America the French and Indian War, was fired May 28, 1754, and the command was given by a youthful Virginia lieutenant colonel then only 22 years old.

Voltaire, a great French essayist, said, "Such was the complication of political interests that a cannon shot fired in America could give the signal that set Europe in a blaze."

To which Parkman added, "Not quite. It was not a cannon shot, but a volley from the hunting pieces of a few backwoodsmen, commanded by a Virginia youth, George Washington."

In spite of his youth, Washington, six feet two inches tall, with steel-gray eyes and a handsome, serious face, had shown such promise as a soldier that he attracted the attention of Robert Dinwiddie, who governed Virginia. When Dinwiddie became concerned over the advances of the French into what he considered English territory, he chose the tall young officer as the best man to carry a message to the French. Thus it might be said that it was Dinwiddie who started Washington on his great career.

Many years before, English representatives had made a treaty with the Iroquois by which those Indians ceded all the Ohio Valley, which they claimed "by right of conquest." By virtue of that treaty England considered the area, containing the present states of Ohio, Indiana, Michigan, Wisconsin, and parts of Illinois and Pennsylvania, as English territory. Of course it was occupied chiefly by the Indian allies of the French. But not until the French began building forts in it did Dinwiddie take action.

He dispatched Washington and a few companions, with what amounted to a challenge and a threat, to the French commandant of the newly built Fort Le Boeuf, demanding that he withdraw his forces. The commandant, Jacques Legardeur de Saint-Pierre, rejected the ultimatum and Washington began the long and dangerous journey home. Twice he almost lost his life on the way — once, when a treacherous Indian guide fired at him, the other time when a raft on which he and a companion were trying to cross the ice-choked Ohio River capsized, and the two of them narrowly escaped drowning, and freezing to death afterward.

For one night he stopped at a rude cabin owned by John Frazier (or Frazer), a trapper, at the mouth of Turtle Creek where it flowed into the Monongahela River. A few miles below, the Monongahela itself merged with the Allegheny River, forming the great Ohio. With the eye of a born soldier, young Washington saw how important the location was, and when he reached Virginia, recommended it as a site for a fort. His judgment was justified. The forks of the Ohio (where Pittsburgh now stands) became one of the great objectives in the war that followed.

Dinwiddie sent a working party to erect a stockade there. Then — too late — he dispatched Washington, now a lieutenant colonel, with two companies of Virginia frontiersmen to guard them. The French had moved with speed. Finding the English fort being built, they drove off the working party, destroyed the crude stockade, and erected on the spot a strong fort of their own, which they named Duquesne, after their commander.

Washington, following as rapidly as possible, was still some distance from the scene when he met the working party in its retreat. He advanced, and at Great Meadows (near Uniontown, Pennsylvania) laid out a crude fort, on which his men set to work. Then, hearing that a party of French was lurking in the vicinity, he made a night march with forty men, and just at dawn, May 28, 1754, surprised the enemy's camp. It was then that Washington gave the order to fire — the order which sent those first historic shots from the guns of his men.

It was a brief little battle. Washington lost one killed and two wounded; the French, 10 killed and 21 captured, only one of them escaping to carry the news to Fort Duquesne. Among the dead was the French commander, the Sieur de Jumonville.

Unhappily, Washington's first victory was quickly followed by his first defeat. As soon as Jumonville's fate was learned at Duquesne, a heavy force was sent hotfoot after the Virginian. They found him and his men working on the fort he had previously started at Great Meadows, which he named Fort Necessity. There, after an all-day fight in a heavy rain against overwhelming odds, Washington, for the first and last time, surrendered to an enemy. He was to know defeat later, but never capitulation. On this occasion he was allowed to march out with his men and their arms. It was a dejected young officer who led his handful back to Virginia, and reported 30 killed and 70 wounded in his brief campaign.

Although the first effort to control the forks of the Ohio had failed, the attention of Britain's high command in London had been forcibly called to the importance of Washington's strategic choice. Despite the fact that Britain and France were nominally at peace, it was resolved to send a force of sufficient strength to capture the French fort there against any resistance the generals could imagine. The difficulty, as it turned out, was that the generals were short on imagination.

On February 25, 1755, the ship-of-the-line *Centurion* arrived at Hampton Roads, Virginia. It carried General Edward Braddock, a spit-and-polish soldier who had been commander of the famed Coldstream Guards. Later transports brought two

regiments of British regulars, to which were added two regiments recruited in the colonies, totaling, with the baggage and artillery trains, 2200 men — quite an army for the time and area, and in a period of supposed peace, as well. With this force, the British commander set out on a toilsome march toward Fort Duquesne.

Much has been said in criticism of Braddock. He was scornful of the Virginia militia; in fact, of all colonials in general. But he was brave, and recognized soldierly qualities. He at once offered Washington a position on his own staff, and Washington accepted.

To transport his cannon and supply wagons through the miles of thickly grown forest (roughly along where today's U.S. Route 40 lies) Braddock was compelled to build a road. Though 600 men constantly felled trees and cleared the way ahead, for much of his march he averaged only two miles a day. It was June 18 before he reached Great Meadows. There he received a report that 500 French regulars were marching to reinforce Fort Duquesne. At that, Braddock took Washington's advice to leave the heavy baggage and march with a "flying column" of about 1200 men, light artillery, and pack train. Though he was ill, Washington accompanied this advance.

Thus far, although Indian scalping parties lurked in the woods to cut off stragglers from the column, there had been no real opposition. With supreme confidence Braddock pushed on. He forded the Monongahela River on July 9, only a few miles from the French fort, his troops in parade marching order, a brave and splendid show, the regulars in red coats, the Virginians in blue, the irregulars in their hunting shirts, the bands playing.

At Fort Duquesne the French were almost in a panic. The commander, Contrecoeur, was about to abandon it and retreat, when a subordinate, young Chevalier de Beaujeu, begged to be allowed to make at least some effort to resist. Permission was granted, and Captain Beaujeu went to the Indians, camped closely around the fort, to seek warriors. He got them, not only by his own persuasions, but through the influence of an Ottawa chief about thirty-five years old named Pontiac, who was to win bloody fame in history years later as the leader in the great Indian uprising called the Pontiac War.

Barrels of gunpowder and musket balls were opened before the gates of the fort and the savages

helped themselves. Then Beaujeu set forth with 250 Frenchmen and 647 Indians — fewer than 900 men, mostly undisciplined savages — to meet the force of 1200 British soldiers.

Of the French, 50 were regulars, the rest bush rangers. About two-thirty in the afternoon, Colonel Thomas Gage, commanding Braddock's advance, saw those regulars directly ahead. A young man in a hunting shirt, but wearing the polished silver gorget of a French officer, was leading them.

He was Beaujeu — for one splendid moment of glory, the central figure in the forest drama. Lifting his hat, he cried *"Vive le Roi!"* ("Long live the King!") and gave the order to fire. In the crash of French muskets several English fell. But Gage was a stout fighter. The heavy answering volley of his men thundered out. Alas, for brave Beaujeu! At this, the first moment of battle, he fell dead.

Some of his men also were down. The French regulars gave ground and the Canadian irregulars fled. But not the Indians. Slipping around the left of the British column, about 300 of them hid in a ravine choked with timber on that side. Others occupied a low forested hill to the right and the ground at its foot, every painted warrior in his own ambush.

Captain M. Dumas, who took command at Beaujeu's death, rallied his soldiers, and with some of the Indians made a stand at the head of the British column. Braddock's light artillery wheeled into line and let go a thundering salvo that rose above the rattle of musketry.

The British van halted. By now the woods were so filled with powder smoke that it was difficult to see. Up hurried the regulars in their brilliant red coats, bayonets flashing, men cheering. They swung into formation as they had been trained, as all

European soldiers were trained. But close-order formation was one they never should have taken. This was no warfare such as they had known, or the British generals in London could have imagined. It was forest fighting, and that day they learned a bitter, bloody, tragic lesson.

For the first time Braddock and his fine regulars were hearing that blood-curdling wolf howl, the Indian war whoop. From both sides of the column it resounded, and the guns never ceased speaking, as British soldiers fell.

In the smoke of battle, which with the thick woods obscured everything, the troops could see nothing of their foes. Blindly they fired volleys — at the trees. And they died bravely, as the British always die, but futilely, under the withering fire from the ravines and the hill.

Vainly the excited Braddock tried to keep them in some kind of order, but in their confusion they huddled together like sheep, discharging their volleys wildly and melting under the Indian sharpshooting.

Knowing Indian habits, some of the Virginians ran ahead to the shelter of some fallen trees to return the enemy's fire. Confused, and seeing the smoke of their guns, the badly rattled regulars shot into them, killing some 50 Virginians — their best fighters in this kind of battle.

Washington strove to advise Braddock; the general would not listen. With magnificent courage but little judgment, he insisted on holding his men in their lines, exposed to a storm of lead to which they had no way of successfully replying. Not until five hours had passed, in which he lost 63 of his 89 officers and the ground was covered with the red uniforms of his slain men, did he at last order retreat.

At this point Washington was the only staff officer left on his feet. That day he had two horses shot from under him and his clothing was riddled with musket balls; yet he was unwounded.

Demoralized, the British began a retreat which presently became a rout. And then, with his men fleeing, Braddock fell, shot through the body and dying. Washington and a Captain Stewart carried him after the army and across the river, where the pursuit mercifully ceased.

Everything was lost — artillery, baggage, 25,000 pounds sterling in coin, all of Braddock's papers, and nearly 900 men. Only a few of the wounded

escaped, the Indians killing any found living on the field. Twelve captured British soldiers were driven back to Fort Duquesne and tortured to death under its walls while the French looked on.

It was the Indians who won the victory — one of their greatest ever over white soldiers. The French, to be sure, were in the battle, but they themselves admitted the Indians fought on their own plan, cutting Braddock's army to pieces after all but a few of the French fled. The Indians suffered a loss of 60 warriors, mostly wounded, and the French 20 men, one of whom was the heroic young Chevalier de Beaujeu.

Braddock died on the retreat home and was buried near Washington's old Fort Necessity. The young Virginian himself carried official word to the Governor of Virginia, telling of perhaps the worst disaster up to that time ever suffered by a British army.

The French and Indians were to learn a lesson, too: that however gravely wounded was the British Lion, it only returned more fiercely to the fray, colonies and mother country alike, until victory as last was won.

The fire kindled on the American frontier spread. A year after Braddock's defeat, England formally went to war with France in the conflict known as the Seven Years' War. That brought well-drilled armies from both nations to America, for each recognized that this time the issue between them must be fought to the finish.

Unprotected, the frontiers of Virginia and Pennsylvania suffered terribly after Braddock's defeat. The wild tribes of the Ohio country, encouraged by their stunning triumph and aided now by the Delawares and Shawnees, who hitherto had been friendly to the English, made a waste of terror, destruction, and death on the border. Dumas, now commanding at Duquesne, boasted that through his dealings with the Indians, "The enemy has lost far more since the battle than on the day of his defeat."

And Washington, left with a few hundred irregulars to the impossible task of guarding 700 miles of undefended frontier against swarming hordes of savages, wrote despairingly to the governor: "The supplicating tears of the women, and the moving petitions of the men, melt me into such deadly sorrow, that I do solemnly declare, if I know my own mind, I could offer myself a willing sacrifice to the butchering enemy, provided it would contribute to the people's ease."

Meantime a real military genius, the Marquis de Montcalm, took command of the French in America, and at once made his presence felt. In a lightning dash he captured and reduced to ashes the English fort and trading post at Oswego on Lake Ontario. Next he turned his attention to the great natural waterway between Canada and the colonial population centers, by way of the Richelieu River, Lakes Champlain and George, and the Hudson River — a convenient way to move armies by water transportation.

The French had forts at Crown Point and Ticonderoga, and the English had Fort William Henry at the southern end of Lake George. Ticonderoga long had been a starting point for scalping parties against the English, and futile efforts had been made to capture it.

Now Montcalm took the initiative. With 6000 soldiers and 1600 Indians, part by land and part in bateaux (flat-bottomed boats) and canoes, he started south on Lake George to attack Fort William Henry. Lieutenant Colonel Monro, a brave Scottish soldier, defended the fort for days against the attacks of besieging forces many times greater than his. But at length, on August 9, 1757, he surrendered, on condition that his people be permitted to return safely home.

On the next day, August 10, when the garrison marched out, there occurred what many have called a blot on the career of Montcalm, although he probably could not have prevented it. As the soldiers, with their women and children appeared, the Indian allies of the French fell suddenly on the column, and a sickening and brutal massacre followed.

Montcalm and his officers tried, sometimes at the risk of their lives, to stop the slaughter. But they could do nothing with the blood-maddened savages. Nobody knows how many died, because hundreds were carried off as captives. Montcalm recovered about 400 of the prisoners, but at least 200 persons were never heard from again.

After destroying Fort William Henry, Montcalm returned to Ticonderoga, where he later heavily defeated a British attack by the incapable General James Abercrombie in one of the bloodiest battles of the war. Meantime, General Jeffrey Amherst and General James Wolfe — who was as brilliant as Montcalm himself — partly restored the situation by capturing Louisbourg, and thus obtained command of the mouth of the St. Lawrence.

But these were operations of white armies, and we are concerned with the Indian phases of this war. The flag of France still floated over Duquesne. As long as it remained there, the American frontier was open to Indian raids, continually inspired by the French.

A brilliant feat by an American officer suddenly changed the outlook of the war. On August 26, 1758, Lieutenant Colonel John Bradstreet, a New England man, with a force of provincials and Oneida warriors crossed Lake Ontario in whaleboats and during the night quietly surrounded Fort Frontenac.

For once the French were completely surprised. They did not dream an enemy could penetrate so far and so secretly, and in such force. The commander, Noyon, surrendered next morning. Though the Oneidas begged Bradstreet to let them kill and scalp the prisoners — about 110 men — he sternly forbade it, showing far better control over his Indians than had Montcalm, and satisfied them with as much of the loot as they could carry.

This bold, almost bloodless stroke, was enormously important. Bradstreet captured nine vessels, carrying from eight to eighteen guns — the entire French naval force on the lake. Huge quantities of provisions, munitions, and Indian goods, intended to supply the western posts, fell into his hands, also 76 pieces of artillery. The cannon and all the supplies that could not be carried away were destroyed, the fort leveled to the ground, and the vessels, after first bearing the captured supplies and munitions to the mouth of the Oswego River, were burned.

Loss of Frontenac was disastrous to the French. Some of their most valuable allies, Indian tribes which had at first been inflamed by the victories at William Henry and Ticonderoga, deserted them. As they no longer received gifts to which they were accustomed, they now sensed the fall of France in America.

Now a new British expedition began grimly toiling through the forests of Pennsylvania toward Fort Duquesne. Its commander was General John Forbes, a brave and canny soldier, who during this campaign was so sick that he had to be carried in a litter, and died shortly afterward. Yet he kept his forces doggedly progressing on a new road he was making, north of the old Braddock track (near the present Pennsylvania Turnpike).

A pair of fine officers commanded the two divisions of his army — Colonel George Washington, and Colonel Henry Bouquet. The latter was a Swiss soldier of fortune, a veteran of European wars, and a loyal soldier of Britain who had the sense to adapt himself to Indian tactics.

Ligneries, now Commandant at Duquesne, soon felt the pinch caused by the loss of Fort Frontenac. Not only did he lack goods to bribe the Indians to fight for him, but a heroic Moravian missionary, Christian Frederick Post, had done much to destroy French influence.

A whole book could be written about Post's adventures alone. Unarmed, he went into the heart of the hostile Indian country, risking death by torture every day to persuade the tribes to peace. Not only did he have to talk to the savages in the face of their constant threats, but often he had to do so in the presence of French officers, who urged the Indians to kill him, and even placed a large price on his life. All these dangers, however, he escaped; and his sincerity and calm reasoning, coupled with the staggering blow the French had suffered, brought about the neutrality of the Delawares, Shawnees, and some the western tribes.

Yet there was to be one more Indian victory. A

rash officer of Forbes's army, Major James Grant, with 600 Highlanders and 150 provincials, began what he called "a reconnaissance in force" toward Duquesne. He got his force badly entangled in the forest and on the morning of September 14 the French garrison, with hundreds of Indian warriors, made a sudden onslaught from the woods about. The Highlanders were so confused that they fled — a thing almost unheard of in those fine fighting men.

Fortunately a company of Virginians, under Captain Bullitt, took a position on a hill, allowed the Highlanders to stream past them, then met the pursuing enemy in one of the hottest little engagements of the war. Of his 75 men Bullitt lost 50 killed or wounded, but he stopped the foe. Grant and about 100 of his men were captured, 273 were killed and 42 wounded, but Bullitt saved the rest.

The setback did not discourage the dogged Forbes. Once more his army moved forward, and now Ligneries knew the end was at hand. Camped twelves miles from the fort, on the night of November 24, the British heard the rumbling of explosions. Next day, advance parties found Duquesne blown up and burned, the French all gone.

Washington, now twenty-seven years old, led the

detachment that entered what was left of the fort, and saw the English colors at last raised over the site of continental importance which he had selected as vital five years before.

Grant's defeat was the last Indian victory in the French and Indian War. The following year, in September, Major Robert Rogers, commander of Rogers' Rangers, in a brilliant raid during which he and his men underwent great hardships and suffering, destroyed the Indian town of St. Francis, gathering place of Abnaki and Caghnawaga raiders against the English, killed 200 Indians, and burned their village to the ground.

Thereafter it was a matter of white armies engaging: Wolfe's historic storming of Quebec, when both he and the gallant Montcalm lost their lives, and the capture of Niagara and Montreal by Amherst.

The fall of Fort Duquesne sealed those two events. By 1760 France had been ousted from Canada, and an expedition led by Rogers and his rangers was taking over all the western forts about the Great Lakes. Out of this was to grow a new era of bloodshed and the rise of another great war leader among the Indians.

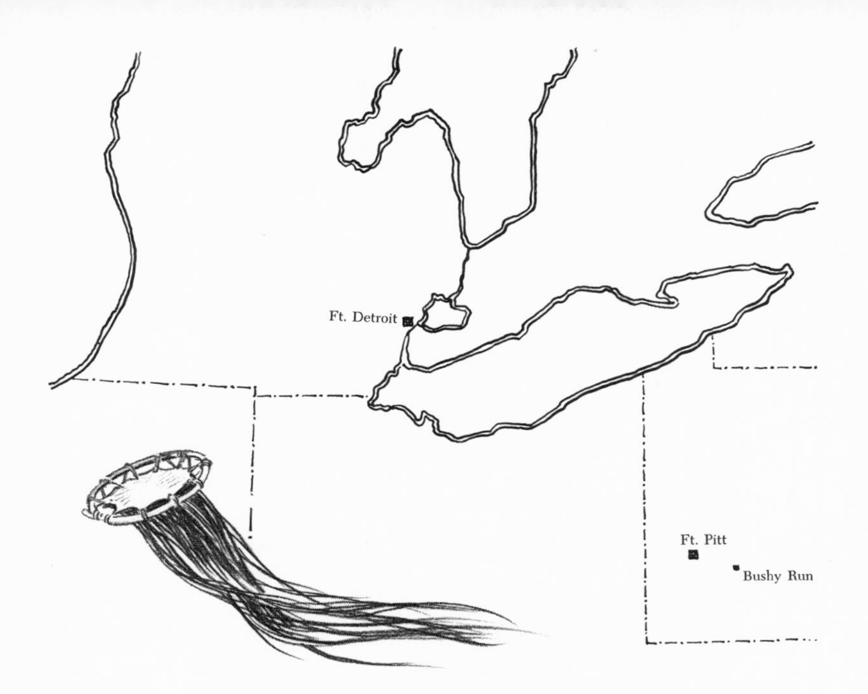

The Dream of Pontiac | 6

IN AN INDIAN VILLAGE on the banks of the Ecorse River, fifteen miles from Fort Detroit, an immense council of chiefs and warriors was being held the morning of April 27, 1763.

This was no ordinary tribal meeting, for in the huge circle squatted representatives of tribes a thousand miles apart: Crees and Nipissings from the far north; Chickasaws from the lower Mississippi; and almost all the tribes in between — wild Chippewas, Wyandots (survivors of the Hurons), Potawatomies, Winnebagos, Sauks and Foxes, Kickapoos, ferocious Senecas and Cayugas from the Iroquois confederacy, Miamis, Shawnees, Delawares, and Ottawas. Every warrior was vivid with war paint, decorated with feathers or horned headdresses, and sitting attentive, silent and grim.

For hours orators had been speaking, but now came the climax as one chief rose. He was not above middle height, but his figure was muscular and athletic. His complexion was dark, his features bold and stern, his bearing commanding. Everyone there knew of him — Pontiac, the great Chief of the Ottawas, possessor of all the Indian talents.

He had been one of the leaders, perhaps *the* leader, in the defeat of Braddock. Elsewhere he had fought for the French; and Montcalm, the French general, presented him the full uniform of a French officer, which Pontiac wore on a few occasions. Now, however, he was dressed in the costume of his people, plumed and painted as for war.

When he began to speak, it was with the deep voice and flaming eloquence of a born orator; and his hearers drank in every word, for what he was proposing to them was so radical and daring that only he among them all could possibly have conceived of it.

Pontiac

First he recited the grievances of the Indians. The English, who now occupied Canada and the Ohio Valley, were not the friends the French had been, he said. No longer were gifts of guns, ammunition, blankets, pipes, and other articles lavished as in the good French times. Worse, Indians who visited forts where once they had been honored guests, now were subjected to insults, and often thrown out. Furthermore, the country was overrun with English traders, many of them scoundrels, who cheated the Indians, dishonored their women, and brought drunkenness into their camps.

Then, his voice rising, Pontiac told his listeners

why he had summoned them there. It was a plan he had slowly matured over two long years of pondering and persuasion. In its simplest form, this was what he proposed: a simultaneous attack by all the different tribes on every fort in the lake and Ohio country, in which all were to be destroyed at once. The forts were to be taken by stratagem or surprise, the settlements overwhelmed by fire and tomahawk. The time was set by a certain phase of the moon.

Nobody but Pontiac could possibly have welded those divergent and often hostile tribes into one force, but for the time being bitter hatreds were forgotten under the spell of his personality and as one man the chiefs and warriors agreed to his scheme — to wipe out every white man west of the Allegheny Mountains, and make those mountains and the Ohio River the frontiers of a realm for Indians only.

Having finished with a final burst of eloquence that left his audience in fanatical excitement and eagerness, he dismissed them to return to their respective countries, and carry out his plan.

What happened thereafter was like a dreadful nightmare. Almost as by a single blow, the forts at Michilimackinac, Sault Ste. Marie, Green Bay, St. Joseph, Ouitenon, Miami, Sandusky, Presque Isle,

Le Boeuf, and Venango fell. Some, like Presque Isle, were taken by storm. Others, like Michilimackinac, were captured by stratagem.

At Michilimackinac, the Chippewas and Sauks invited the garrison to watch a game of "ball play" — a rough and exciting sport, the forerunner of modern lacrosse, played with rackets and a ball. Unsuspecting, the soldiers watched the racing, yelling contestants, until suddenly the ball rose like a meteor, and as if by accident soared within the walls of the fort. Instantly both sides of Indians rushed after it, whooping, and the soldiers, thinking it perfectly natural, allowed them to do so. Once inside, the warriors turned on the garrison and massacred all but a very few, who, with the commander, Major Etherington, were held as prisoners.

Most of the other garrisons overwhelmed were slaughtered or tortured to death. The handful at the little fort on Green Bay was saved by a curious circumstance. One great Indian people had been visited by Pontiac's envoys in vain: the Sioux, who were reported to have 30,000 warriors. Their most hated enemies were the Chippewas, and they would have nothing of a scheme in which those foes played a part.

Instead of joining Pontiac, the Sioux sent a chief to the Menominees, who lived around Green Bay, with a brief ultimatum: "Protect the English garrison, or the Sioux will come and wipe you out!"

As a result of that haughty message, the Menominees not only allowed Lieutenant Gorell and his 17 men to leave peacefully, but undertook to escort them. In bateaux guarded by 90 warriors in canoes, Gorell's party set off up the bay. Near its mouth a Chippewa war party was reported, and the Menominees stripped for battle, ready to fight for the Englishmen. The Chippewas, however, refrained from attacking.

Crossing Lake Michigan, they stopped at an Ottawa village near Michilimackinac, where the Menominees found Major Etherington and eight other survivors of the surprise attack, and — hard as it is to believe — persuaded the Ottawas to free them. With this added party, they paddled across Lake Huron, and by way of Georgian Bay, French River, Lake Nipissing, and several portages reached the Ottawa River, down which they passed, delivering their charges safely at Montreal.

Though he succeeded in his thunderbolt attack against the smaller forts, Pontiac failed in surprising his two main objectives — Fort Detroit, which controlled the water traffic in the Great Lakes system, and Fort Pitt (built on the ruins of Fort Duquesne), which guarded the frontier.

His own plan against Detroit was foiled when a Chippewa girl, who was in love with Major Henry Gladwin, the commander, told the latter that on May 7 Pontiac intended to enter the fort on a supposedly peaceful mission, with 60 braves, each of whom would carry a loaded gun under his blanket.

Gladwin had his men stand to arms, and Pontiac at first glance saw his plan had failed. After smoking and talking, he withdrew with his braves. At once Pontiac's swarming warriors began a blistering fire on the fort, which they kept up for six hours, while all the English who dwelled in the little settlement about the fort were massacred, although the French Canadians there were not molested.

Major Campbell and Lieutenant McDougal, sent to treat with Pontiac, were seized, and Campbell later was tortured to death. A relief expedition from Niagara, led by Lieutenant Cuyler and consisting of 96 men convoying boats loaded with provisions and ammunition, was cut off near the mouth of the Detroit River by Wyandots. Only two boatloads of men, in one of which was the wounded Cuyler, escaped to carry news of the loss to Fort Niagara. The other soldiers were killed, except for three who by a bold dash reached Detroit.

It was July before help finally arrived — 22 barges, carrying several cannon, ammunition, and supplies, and bearing 280 men, numbering among them the redoubtable Robert Rogers and 20 of his rangers. Commanding this expedition was Captain James Dalzell. A fog helped the convoy ascend the Detroit River, but presently it lifted and the savages opened fire. In running the gantlet, 15 men were killed or wounded, but the garrison was rejoiced at the arrival of these welcome reinforcements.

Dalzell was hot to attack Pontiac's village, which the chief had coolly established only three miles north of the fort and on the same side of the river. At last he got Gladwin's reluctant permission. At two o'clock, the morning of July 31, 1763, the rash captain set out with 250 men.

Halfway to the Ottawa camp the soldiers began to cross a bridge over Parent's Creek (since called Bloody Run). In the darkness rose the wild war-whoop, and a blast of gunfire knocked down half the advance guard of 25 men. Appalled, the survivors fell back. Dalzell rushed forward, sword in hand and shouting encouragement, to rally his troops.

He led a charge across the bridge, but the Indians simply faded into the trees and bushes, from which their guns sent a continual hail of death. It was retreat or die. With Dalzell bravely bringing up the rear, the men began their return to the fort. Twice the captain was wounded, as guns blazed in the night on both sides of the road. At last, when trying to save a wounded sergeant, he was killed.

Along the way some Indians kept up a deadly fire from an empty house. Rogers and his rangers broke into it, drove out the savages, and from it covered the retreat with their rifles, being the last to follow into the fort, after six hours of fighting.

So ended Dalzell's scheme "to catch Pontiac napping," with a loss of 59 men, including Dalzell himself. The Indians lost no more than 15 or 20.

And still the siege continued — a siege without parallel in the history of American Indian warfare. For almost five months, from early May to late September, Pontiac besieged the place. No other Indian chief ever showed such grim perseverance and determination.

Fort Pitt had during this time proved as hard a nut to crack as Detroit. No chief of Pontiac's stature was there to direct the assault. Thirsty for blood and longing for scalps, the young warriors of the Delawares and Shawnees began a series of premature raids, killing at least a hundred traders and many settlers in isolated cabins.

Thus warned, the garrison destroyed all buildings about the fort, to prevent their being used as cover by the enemy. Fort Pitt was well built. It was five-sided, with walls partly of brick, and was armed with a number of cannon. Within it the whites in the vicinity were gathered for safety.

When the attack came on the night of July 26 it

was in the form of a continuous heavy fire of small arms. The Indians dug pits from which to shoot, and a few men fell on the ramparts. For six entire days and nights the whizzing bullets sped against the walls, while fire arrows arched over the rampart and kept the garrison busy extinguishing blazes. Though the women and children were put in places of safety, the men were nearly exhausted by constant duty on the parapets.

Then, suddenly as it began, the attack ceased. Relieved but fearful, the defenders wondered where the Indians had gone, and why.

There was a reason. Marching along the road built by Forbes in 1758 was Colonel Bouquet, who had distinguished himself with Washington in the capture of Duquesne. He had with him only about 500 men, but they were battalions of two famous regiments, the Highland Black Watch and the Royal Americans.

By August 5, Bouquet reached Bushy Run, about twenty-five miles from Fort Pitt. It was an area of bloody history. A few miles away Braddock's force had been destroyed, and still nearer Grant had suffered his defeat. Bouquet knew Indians were in the vicinity because scalping parties had skulked about his column for days. But early that afternoon, heavy firing and the usual wild yelling at the front heralded a major battle. The Indians who had been besieging Fort Pitt were attacking him.

Like the howling of wild beasts in the forest, their war cries came from every quarter as they took advantage of their snake-like mobility to surround the army, pouring upon it a constant fire. Bouquet was no Braddock. He ordered his men to lie flat rather than stand and fire by volleys. Even so, the Highlanders and Royal Americans suffered severely. By nightfall, 60 men and several officers were dead or wounded.

When the battle lulled at dark, Bouquet retreated to a little hill, placing his men by companies in a circle, with a crude little enclosure of sacks of flour in the center to protect such of the wounded as had escaped the ruthless scalping knife.

He supposed that night would be his last, as he said in a report he wrote to his superior, General Jeffrey Amherst. Yet he did not stop planning and thinking in those dark hours. His only hope of victory was to bring his will-o'-the-wisp enemies to a stand where his men could get at them. So that night he formed a daring plan.

Next morning the Indians resumed their attack on his haggard band, and for four hours the firing continued, the red men growing increasingly bold. Watching this, at the right moment Bouquet gave the word for a crafty move in which he had schooled his soldiers during the night. All at once two companies of Highlanders fell back, as if retreating, and left a gap in the line. Exultantly the Indians leaped forward in a yelling mass to cut the center out of the white army, and charged straight into the gap.

But the Highlanders, far from retreating, merely hid in a ravine where they were not seen. Now with yells as fierce as any the Indians had given, they drew their claymores (basket-hilted swords with which Highland rank and file were then armed) and sprang forward to kill. At the same time the companies on either side of the gap charged in. Caught in the jaws of this amazing trap, the Indians simply melted. Many were cut down by the furious Highlanders. The others fled, leaving their dead behind.

Bouquet's loss was 115 men and officers, killed or wounded, but he had crushed the Indians and saved Fort Pitt. The Battle of Bushy Run, one of the most brilliant and hard-fought in all the Indian wars,

was the decisive blow in the Pontiac War.

At this time Pontiac learned that the French, on whom he had counted, would not help him. His dream of expelling the white men was shattered. Brokenhearted, he offered peace, and his tribes buried the hatchet.

As for the great Pontiac himself, he was murdered by a tomahawk in the hands of a Kaskaskia Indian, in April 1769. The killer had been bribed with a barrel of liquor, by an English trader named Williamson, to do the foul deed.

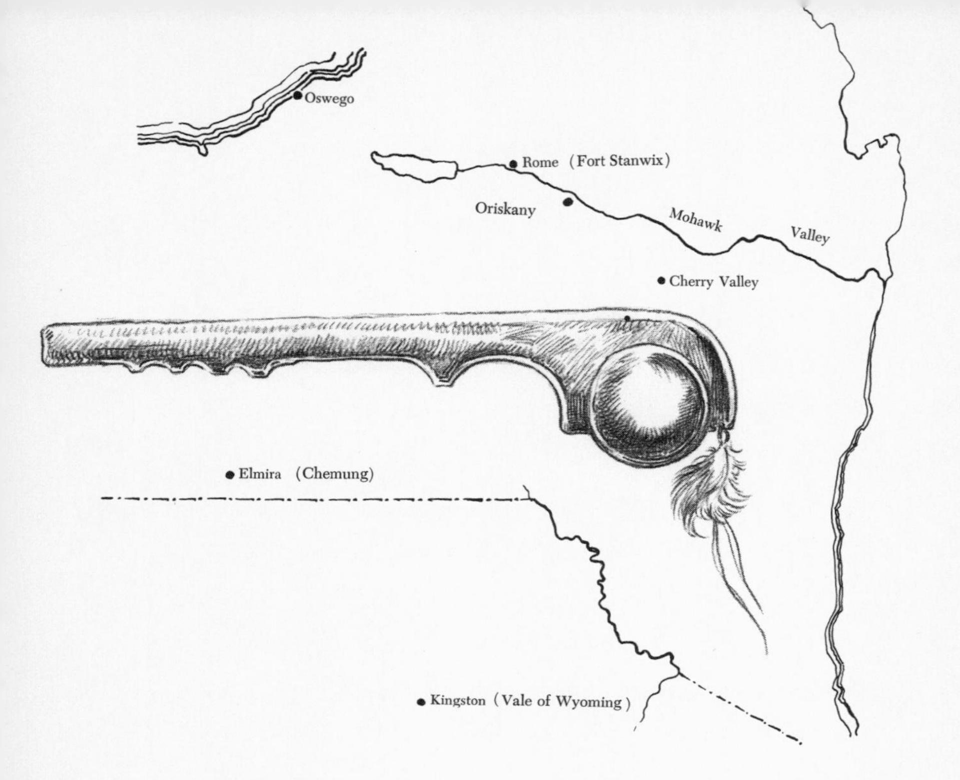

7 Tories and Iroquois

EVEN BEFORE the Pontiac War, American frontiersmen were pressing far into the Indian country so long disputed.

D.BOON
CilleD A BAR ON
ThE TREE
in yEAR
1760

That inscription, found carved on an aged beech tree, would indicate that Daniel Boone, greatest of the pioneers, was in Kentucky as early as 1760. This has been disputed. Yet it is very possible, for in that year he was twenty-five or twenty-six years old, a veteran "long hunter." The presence of such men and their families created endless trouble with the Indians, and the record of ambushes, raids, and fights in the forests can never be completed, for simple lack of a record of their numberless events.

The frontier developed men of every type. Boone ranks as a true forest nobleman. The opposite end of the scale was the notorious Simon Girty, son of a drunken Irish trader, adopted by the Senecas, a provincial soldier for a time, then a deserter who went back to the savages, and became more savage than they in bloody exploits and inhuman tortures of prisoners.

It was during the American Revolution, however, that the Indians again became a real menace.

The Iroquois in 1775 had been reduced by their wars so that even with adopted prisoners in their ranks they numbered fewer than 1500 warriors. Sir William Johnson, Commissioner to the Iroquois and married to a Mohawk girl, had kept all of them except the Senecas from the warpath during the Pontiac uprising. But as it became apparent that the colonies would rebel against King George III, he was so torn between his loyalty to his king and his friendship toward the colonists that, knowing the Iroquois would go either way at his word, he secluded himself and died suddenly in 1774, by his own hand, it is believed.

His son, Sir John Johnson, and his neighbors, Guy Johnson, Colonel John Butler, and the latter's son, Captain Walter Butler, were thorough Tories who had no scruples about using Indians against their neighbors on the frontier. This was easy, since the Mohawks resented the settlers, chiefly German-Americans, who were pushing up the Mohawk Valley with their farms. Besides, Molly Brant (the Mohawk woman who was Sir William's widow), had a brother educated as a member of the family by her late husband, who was an influential chief of the Iroquois — Joseph Brant.

Brant's Indian name was Thayendanegea. He was thirty-three years old, had been to London, could read, write, and speak English well, and had fought for the British since he was only thirteen years old. A tall, dignified man, polite in manner, he was quite handsome, especially in his keen eyes and bold chin and nose.

Joseph Brant

These five men — four English-American Tories and a Mohawk chief — succeeded in winning to the English cause most of the Iroquois. Only the Oneidas and part of the Tuscaroras refused to join them.

At first there were a few minor raids in northern New York. But in the spring of 1777, handsome Lieutenant Colonel Barry St. Leger of the British army, a veteran of the French and Indian War, appeared at Oswego. There he began forming an army of Tories and Indians. His orders were to march with this force up the Oswego River and down the Mohawk. Near Albany he was expected to join General John Burgoyne, who with the main British army was then beginning his campaign "to cut the colonies in two."

With that, murderous action began. St. Leger started his march with 1200 men — Tories under the Johnsons and Butlers and Iroquois under Brant. The Indians burned houses, ran off livestock, and killed and scalped as they advanced, until they encountered a stubborn Dutchman, Colonel Peter Gansevoort, with 550 men at Fort Stanwix (where Rome, New York, now stands). Stanwix was almost a ruin, yet it was defended with such courage that St. Leger was brought to a halt while he besieged the place for three weeks.

To the rescue marched old General Nicholas Herkimer, also a veteran of the French and Indian War, but an American leader now with about 800 Tryon County militia. He had at one time tried to get Brant to join the patriot side, but had failed. Now as he neared Stanwix, he managed to get a messenger through to Gansevoort with a plan to attack St. Leger from both sides at the same time, the signal to be three cannon shots from the fort.

On the night of August 5, Herkimer halted eight miles from Stanwix to await the signal. His officers thought him too cautious. After a heated argument, in which the general was accused of everything from cowardice to outright treason, he at length, against his better judgment, ordered an advance the morning of August 6.

It was exactly what the enemy wanted. About two miles west of Oriskany Creek, in a marshy ravine choked with timber, the Americans were suddenly beset on all sides by Iroquois and Tories. A battle ensued, so bloody and bitter as rarely to have been equaled.

Early, a bullet killed Herkimer's horse and shattered the old general's leg. Ordering his saddle placed under a tree, he sat on it, calmly lit his pipe, and directed the defense. Again and again the Indians charged, but his men, raw though they were, fought like veterans under the eye of their leader. Seeing that often when one of his soldiers fired, a savage would rush forward and tomahawk him before he could reload, Herkimer put two men behind each tree, one to shoot while the other reserved his fire, with a ball ready to stop such tactics.

It seemed that human courage and endurance could hardly withstand any longer the constantly growing losses and the ferocious pressure of the overwhelming enemy force. Then, as if to make still more terrible the already deadly conflict with its piercing yells, its roar of gunfire, and its cries of

the wounded, a thunderstorm burst over the scene. This came with such violence of lightning, rain, and wind that it awed both sides into suspending the battle temporarily.

Actually it saved Herkimer's men. When the wild storm passed and fighting began again, the men from Fort Stanwix arrived and the Tories and Iroquois retreated from the field. Brave old Herkimer died from loss of blood. Of his men 200 were dead and twice as many wounded or taken prisoner. But Oriskany has been called "the turning point of the Revolution." It was the first setback of the Burgoyne campaign, in which that general eventually surrendered his army in the decisive siege of Saratoga.

At the appearance of a force under Benedict Arnold (not yet a traitor), St. Leger was driven out of the campaign, all the way back to Oswego. His losses had been greater than Herkimer's. Smarting from their defeat, the Iroquois, in the retreat, tortured many of their prisoners to death. They craved revenge, and Black Snake, Little Beard, and Cornplanter left red trails of slaughter across the Unadilla Hills in months following.

Most terrible of the Iroquois massacres were those in the Vale of Wyoming (near Kingston, Pennsylvania), June 3 to 6, 1778, and in Cherry Valley (Otsego County, New York), November 11, 1778.

The Wyoming massacre has been called "the surpassing horror of the Revolution." When John Butler with 900 Indians and 200 Tories stole down on the valley, June 3, most of the able-bodied men were away with Washington's army. Colonel Zebulon Butler (a patriot cousin of the Tory leader) happened to be home on furlough when word was brought of the oncoming horde. Hurriedly gathering the families at Forty Fort, north of Kingston, with about 300 old men and boys, he tried to form some sort of a fighting force.

Untrained as they were and armed with ancient fowling pieces and flintlocks, they were full of fight. When reports of Indian atrocities began coming in, they demanded to be led against the enemy. Colonel Butler doubtfully consented, and disaster was the result.

Though outnumbered nearly four to one, the thin American line held, until the Iroquois slipped around the flank and attacked it from the rear. What followed might have been expected — a rout. Mohawks, Senecas, and Cayugas, dropping their guns, bounded in pursuit with only their tomahawks to deal death. Of the Americans 240 were slain.

In the next three terrible days every house in the valley was burned, sometimes, it is said, with the occupants who locked themselves within. "Queen

Esther's Rock" is pointed out as the place where "the fiend of Wyoming" — a mixed-blood Indian squaw named Esther Montour, granddaughter of a French nobleman — in sheer blood-lust killed 16 helpless prisoners who were held by brawny warriors for her murdering tomahawk.

Brant was not present at Wyoming, but he was at the Cherry Valley slaughter, an equally brutal scene. Not a man's life was spared there, and every house was burned but one, which was used to hold the women and children, later taken away as captives.

Dreadful as they were, Wyoming and Cherry Valley had a decisive result. Justly furious, General Washington determined to punish the Iroquois so that they could never recover. The next summer — 1779 — he sent General John Sullivan with 2500 men and General James Clinton with 1500 more to scourge the enemy's country.

Brant tried to draw aside this invasion by raiding Minisink (Orange County, New York), and defeated a small American force there on June 20. But he lost so heavily that he had to retreat. During this time the American generals, refusing to be drawn aside, had marched up the Mohawk Valley.

Brant hastened back, but he could muster no more than 600 warriors against 4000 men. At Chemung and Newtown Creeks (near present Elmira, New York), his Indians and Tories were brushed aside in brief battles. For the first time in all history, the Iroquois were swept from their own country.

Thereafter Sullivan and Clinton ravaged the entire Indian area. Few Iroquois were killed, and the few taken prisoner were well treated. But 40 Indian villages were burned, 160,000 bushels of corn and beans destroyed, countless fruit orchards cut down, and all livestock driven away. The Iroquois were left destitute, their power forever broken. Most of them went over into Canada, where their descendants still live.

Thus did the once terrible Iroquois make their exit from history, with the wailing of their women the only requiem for the departed glories of the great confederation that once held half of eastern America in dread of its slightest frown.

Never again would Indian war disfigure New York and New England. But west of the Allegheny Mountains an ominous new cloud was gathering which would break soon in a bloody storm.

The Greatest Indian Victory | 8

After the Revolution, in spite of the peace treaty, the British kept their garrisons in the border forts, such as Detroit, Oswego, Niagara, Michilimackinac, and Miami — the latter "an invasion of nearly forty miles into United States territory."

Those forts controlled the fur trade of the Great Lakes; British interests, combined with hatred of the new American nation, caused them to supply Indians with weapons, supplies, and other gifts, and keep them stirred up in constant raids against the frontier.

In the south General John Sevier taught a bloody lesson to the Cherokees which they never forgot. In that war a young redheaded lieutenant led some brilliant expeditions against the Indians. His name was Andrew Jackson, and he went on to become one of the mighty figures of our history, the greatest military hero of his day in America, and President of the nation.

Yet in spite of such efforts, on the frontier between 1783 and 1790 more than 1500 men, women, and children were killed, wounded, or carried off by Indians, and much property looted or destroyed.

When George Washington took oath as the first President, April 30, 1789, one of the countless problems confronting him was the question of the Indians, complicated by the attitude of Britain, and the fear that if the tribes were attacked it might bring on another war with that nation. But Washington refused to let the people of the frontiers continue to suffer. On September 30, 1790, he took a calculated risk in sending General Josiah Harmar to defeat the Indian confederacy that had grown up north of the Ohio.

The choice of commander was unfortunate. Harmar had served bravely enough in the Revolution as a subordinate under the very capable General Nathaniel Greene. Given a command of his own, however, he proved to be unimaginative, slow-thinking, and easily fooled by his enemy.

A new Indian military genius had arisen. He was a Miami chief named Little Turtle, thirty-eight years old in 1790. His face was that of a leader, with its large, dark, intensely searching eyes, very high forehead, hooked nose, and wide, grim mouth. It was said of him his manner was so reserved that none of the other chiefs liked him. Nevertheless, his word was never broken, and his knowledge of war was so great that the Indians all obeyed him. One of his underchiefs was Tecumseh, a young Shawnee who though only twenty-two years old already was notable among his people. A second was Red Jacket, a famous Seneca orator. A third was Simon Girty, the cruel white renegade.

With a force of Miamis, Shawnees, Delawares, Wyandots, and a few Iroquois, Little Turtle set out to face Harmar when the latter, with 1435 officers and men, marched from Fort Washington (Cincinnati, Ohio) in October. He found the task to his liking, for Harmar was so much his inferior in strategy that the Miami chief played with him as a child would play with a toy.

First he sent a swift-moving band of warriors to act as a decoy. Harmar swallowed the bait, and detached a "flying column" of 800 militia under Colonel John Hardin to catch those rash Indians. As soon as this column was sufficiently separated from Harmar, it was in trouble.

Along his line of march, Hardin found Indian villages burned and deserted. Fearing he would lose his prey, he rushed forward with such haste that he blundered into a clever trap set by Little Turtle — who at the place had fewer warriors than were in Hardin's command. In the ambush Hardin lost 23 killed, while inflicting hardly a casualty on the Indians. The militia fled and Little Turtle had his first victory.

Not daunted, Harmar received the flying soldiers, calmed them, and marched on. When he reached the Miami River, Little Turtle's warriors were all about him. One night the Indians ran off most of the cavalry horses. So furious was Harmar that he again sent off 500 men under Hardin on a wild goose chase his adversary had marked out for him.

Little Turtle must have smiled. Having for the second time caused his enemy to divide his forces,

he this time turned on the bewildered Harmar himself, on October 22.

In the fight that followed, the small army was punished severely with the loss of 150 men, among whom were three majors. Harmar had had quite enough of Little Turtle. When Hardin rejoined him he retreated hastily to Fort Washington.

The defeat was a heavy blow to American prestige, and Washington knew it must be retrieved. He called General Arthur St. Clair, Governor of the Northwest Territory, to Philadelphia. St. Clair was a brave but aging officer with white hair who was in ill health. He had served well under Washington at the battles of Trenton, Princeton, and elsewhere, and the President trusted him.

Washington knew Indian fighting — he had cut his military eyeteeth on it. As he gave St. Clair command of a new army to invade the Indian country his final warning was very earnest: "Beware of a surprise. You know how the Indians fight, and I repeat, *beware of a surprise!*"

It was October 3, 1791, when St. Clair, with 2000 men, including two regiments of infantry, with artillery and cavalry, set out from Fort Washington. Very slowly he advanced, building and garrisoning forts on the way, until when he reached the Wabash River he had only about 1400 men with him. There, on the evening of November 3, his army went into camp. St. Clair was sick and confined to his tent. The night passed without event. In the morning the drums beat reveille as usual, the troops held roll-call formation, then were dismissed for breakfast.

At this moment Little Turtle struck with the sudden deadliness of a rattlesnake.

Without warning, from the woods where they had been concealed all night, bounded a wave of ferocious, painted, whooping savages. Little Turtle knew just where to hurl his charge. Full on a regiment of militia, ill-trained and ill-officered, the shock fell. Tomahawked and shot down by the terrifying savage horde, the militia broke and ran, throwing into confusion even the regulars, who were forming as fast as they could seize their weapons.

St. Clair was almost captured in his tent by that first screaming Indian rush. A charge by the regulars saved him. Half dressed, his white locks streaming in the air, he took command with the greatest personal bravery.

With the bayonet the regulars pursued the Indians into the forest. This also was a part of Little Turtle's plan. He had warriors planted in places of concealment, from which they blasted the troops, as Braddock had been blasted long before.

As the soldiers stumbled out of the ambush, a second thunderbolt charge by Little Turtle drove in the American left flank. There the artillery was parked. In a few bloody moments almost every artilleryman was killed, and all the cannon put out of commission.

Their flank turned, the death yell in their ears, and the painted foe swarming about them, the bewildered soldiers were pushed into a huddled mass, in which at almost every moment gaps were cut by the sleet of lead from the surrounding trees and underbrush.

Despairing, and knowing all was lost, St. Clair after two hours gave the order to retreat.

Utterly demoralized, his troops threw down guns, knapsacks, everything, in a disgraceful, panic-

stricken rout. Behind them raged the Indians, slaying. They might have killed every one of the white soldiers, had they not stopped to loot the camp. As it was, more than 900 men lay dead on that stricken field. St. Clair escaped on an old baggage mule. It was the greatest military disaster ever suffered by American arms against Indians. It is the solitary American battle which has no name. "St. Clair's Defeat" is the only title by which it is known.

When news of it reached Washington, he cried in passion, "It's all over! St. Clair is defeated! Routed! The officers nearly all killed, the men by the wholesale! The rout complete! Too shocking to think of, *and a surprise in the bargain!*"

Yet he gave St. Clair a fair hearing. The general was exonerated of negligence and lack of courage, but resigned his commission and office.

Putting down the Indian menace had now become a grim necessity. In the crisis Washington turned to General Anthony Wayne, a hero of the Revolution, called "Mad Anthony" because of his fearlessness in battle. Wayne, a tough fighter, forty-six years old in 1791, was so devoted to Washington that he was once quoted as saying, "I would charge into hell, if General Washington gave the command." He had been brilliant during the Revolution, particularly in his capture of Stony Point, a British stronghold, by night, and his daring exploits were a legend in the army.

He was shrewd as well as tempestuous. When he received his orders from his chief he began by enlisting 1000 men, chiefly from the frontiers. Then he drilled them. He was a superb drillmaster, and before he was through with those frontier hunters they were soldiers — a disciplined, hard-fighting unit, proud of the name he gave them, "The Legion of the United States." For uniforms they wore bearskin caps, fringed hunting shirts, and Indian moccasins. They knew how to load their rifles on the run, and were trained to such a fine pitch that even against an imaginary enemy they would leap into icy water in a bayonet charge.

With the Legion — and militia and cavalry raising his force to 3000 men — Wayne marched north in the spring of 1793 along the trail of his predecessors, Harmar and St. Clair. He built Fort Recovery at the site of St. Clair's Defeat, and buried the bones of hundreds of men found there.

Little Turtle, that savage tactician, had been trying every ruse and trick he knew. He sought to cut off detachments, but Wayne was too alert. He attacked Fort Recovery, and was heavily repulsed. His warriors stalked the sentry lines, hoping to find a man asleep, but in vain. His efforts to stampede the troop horses failed.

So impressed was the great Miami that he urged his people to make peace with "the chief that never sleeps." The tribes refused, so Little Turtle prepared to fight. He chose a battlefield ideally suited to his method of fighting.

A few miles from the British-held Fort Miami (Maumee, Ohio), a tornado had at one time swept through the forest, leaving a tangled swath of prostrate trees, over which it seemed impossible for an army to pass. There Little Turtle posted his warriors, and there, August 20, 1794, the Battle of Fallen Timbers was fought.

The Indian leader, to oppose Wayne's 3000 men, had only about 1300 warriors and some 70 Canadian and English rangers. And of these only about 800 actually took part in the fight.

Wayne formed his troops in a double line. The first line, composed of the Legion, was to charge, the second line was to support it, and the mounted volunteers were to sweep around and fall on the Indian rear.

But the fury of the first wave of assault carried all before it. Tecumseh, one of whose brothers was killed at his side, did his utmost to keep his Shawnees in line, and Turkey Track, an Ottawa chief, was killed rallying his braves. The Indians could not stand against the Legion's bayonets.

Over the tangled mass of fallen timbers, the soldiers clambered and leaped, yelling like the Indians themselves. In a few moments Little Turtle's warriors were in retreat. Driven from their defenses, they fled, pursued by the cavalry seven miles to the very walls of Fort Miami. There they expected shelter by the British, but the gates were not opened, and Wayne's horsemen mercilessly cut down all who could not escape.

Fallen Timbers ended a generation of Indian wars. Wayne lost 44 killed and 89 wounded; Little Turtle's loss was three times as great.

The following year, on August 3, 1795, the chiefs signed a treaty of peace at Greenville, Ohio. As he made his mark, Little Turtle said, "I am the last to sign it, and I will be the last to break it."

He was true to his word. Later he visited President Washington at Philadelphia. He died peacefully at Fort Wayne, Indiana, July 14, 1812.

Though the Battle of Fallen Timbers ended the war trail for Little Turtle, it may be said to have been the start of the career of another great Indian, and of his labors which made his name more famous in his time than that of any other member of his race.

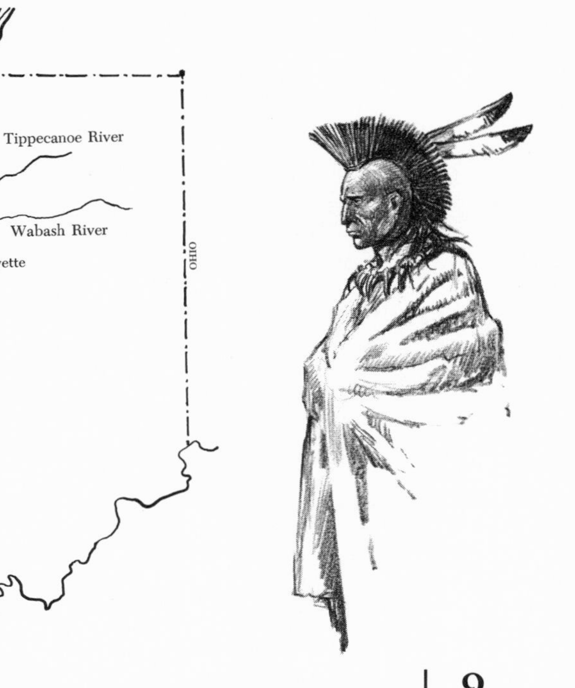

The Fates against Tecumseh | 9

ONE WHO REFUSED to sign the Greenville treaty was Tecumseh, the young Shawnee chief who had fought so bravely at Fallen Timbers. After the battle he went west, and then south, living with various tribes other than his own, to learn their languages and make friends with them.

Certainly Tecumseh was one of the most appealing Indian figures of history. He was handsome, with penetrating eyes and a fine figure, and agile as a wildcat. Not only was he a heroic warrior, but he was one of the greatest orators his race ever produced. His voice was thus described: "It possessed the vibrating resonance of an organ, and, when roused to one of his fiery outbursts, seemed to pulsate through the air with a magnetic power that was irresistible."

His manner was lofty and impressive, and there is no question that he won the admiration of even the white men who knew him. He has been called "the most extraordinary Indian in history." Looking at him today, we must conclude that the brilliance of his personality obscured the fact that he seemed born under an evil star.

Traveling among other tribes was no whim on his part. For early in his life he formed a plan that was colossal in scope. Pontiac was his ideal and model. But in his vision he outstripped even that great Ottawa. Tecumseh's dream was nothing less than a permanent federation — a *nation* — of Indians that would embrace every tribe east of the Mississippi.

To form such a federation was a gigantic and complicated task, since it meant uniting a hundred tribes which were of different customs and districts and were often feuding. But with his wonderfully intense enthusiasm, to which he added an equally magnificent ability in diplomacy and statesmanship, he threw himself into the work — and almost succeeded.

To begin with, he foresaw — long before most white men — that there would soon be another war between Britain and the United States. Statesman that he was, he counted on this war to help him establish his Indian federation, and his people's rights, for he was one of the first to think of all Indians as one people, regardless of tribal or other differences.

Tecumseh's twin brother, Tenskwatawa, was a medicine man. By some means — perhaps through Tecumseh, who had contacts with a few prominent white men — he learned there would be an eclipse of the sun on a certain day. Making a great ceremony of predicting it, he gathered a huge crowd of Indians, and when the sun "died" and then came back to life, the onlookers were seized with intense excitement. The medicine man had now become a "prophet," and as the Shawnee Prophet, he became the head of a religious movement, being regarded by countless savages as a sacred being, and preaching return to the old, primitive life and ways of their ancestors for the purification of their lives and restoration of their race.

All this exactly suited Tecumseh, whose master mind saw how religious enthusiasm could be used to weld the tribes together. With satisfaction he watched people from many tribes gather together and form a great Indian village, known as Prophet's Town, on the Tippecanoe River, a few miles north of the present city of Lafayette, Indiana.

By 1810 his work had so far progressed that he hurled a bold ultimatum right into the teeth of the white man. At a council with General William Henry Harrison, he denied the right of the government to purchase lands *from any single tribe,* since it belonged to *all* Indians, and said that if white aggression continued, he would oppose it with war.

It was an immense step forward in Indian policy, and by this and other acts Tecumseh now had become the most noted Indian in America. But he had no intention of fighting yet — he was waiting for the inevitable conflict with Britain for his great gathering of the united tribes to aid the British and win for themselves security in their country.

So, giving strict orders to his brother that there should be no hostilities in his absence, he went south in 1811 to organize the tribes there.

His wonderful eloquence won to him most of his hearers in the Choctaw, Chickasaw, Creek, and Cherokee villages. And the overpowering impression his personality made, even on those who hesitated, was shown by a strange happening. Leaving a Creek village that had been cool to him, Tecumseh said indignantly, "When I reach Detroit I will stamp my foot, and the very earth shall shake!"

By a remarkable coincidence, the tremendous earthquake of New Madrid, Missouri, took place December 16, 1811, about the time the Creeks computed that he had reached his destination. It was so violent that it caused a great area of ground to sink (creating Reelfoot Lake) and it shook the country for hundreds of miles.

With their houses falling about them, the Creeks rushed out in frantic terror, crying, "Tecumseh has reached Detroit!"

It seemed that the great Shawnee had achieved his purpose. He was jubilant at the thought that his federation was complete and ready to play its decisive part when the British-American war came. Yet at this moment of victory — even before the earthquake convinced the wavering Creeks — his dream was shattered.

While Tecumseh was gone his brother, the Prophet, greedy for personal glory, had disobeyed his orders and busied himself stirring up war spirit among the Indians. So dangerous was the situation that General Harrison marched to the trouble spot with 1000 troops, arriving near Prophet's Town on November 6. Three chiefs, remembering Tecumseh's orders, came to him asking for a conference and promising there would be no hostilities. So Harrison and his men camped about a mile from the village.

The Prophet, however, was less loyal to his brother's commands than the three chiefs. Ambitious and vain, he spent the night working the warriors of his village into a frenzy. Before dawn, November 7, 1811, about 1000 fanatical braves — without leaders, and largely without plan — hurled themselves suddenly on Harrison's camp.

In their first mad assault, they drove in the pickets and charged toward the center of the camp. But Harrison was alert, and his well-trained soldiers had slept fully clad, with their arms beside them.

As the shooting, howling foe came on, they fought back with desperate determination. In the darkness guns lit up the swirling conflict, and fired point-blank with muzzles almost against the bodies of their targets. Bayonet and rifle butt clashed and thudded against tomahawk and war club. Yells, cries, the reports of guns, and thudding of feet filled the night with a terrifying din.

But the Indians could not break the soldiers.

When daylight came, and Harrison could see, he sent his men in a series of disciplined charges that

drove the Indians with bloody losses from the field and scattered them. Then, though he had lost about a third of his army in killed or wounded, he destroyed Prophet's Town before returning to Vincennes.

Tecumseh arrived a few days later to hear news that to him must have been terrible. The Battle of Tippecanoe had upset his entire plan. His warriors had been wasted in a useless and disastrous night battle, without proper leadership. Worse, all through the Indian country the word was running that it was no use to fight the white man and that the great alliance had failed.

Poor Tecumseh — imagine his anguish and disappointment at seeing his whole great dream wrecked! One can sympathize with his fury and despair, when later he confronted the Prophet, and "seized his brother by the hair and almost shook the life out of him." But it was too late to change things. What made it even more heartbreaking to Tecumseh was the fact that the War of 1812, the British-American conflict he had clearly foreseen and on which he had counted, began the very next June.

From that day Tecumseh's life was an unhappy anticlimax. He joined the British, with hundreds of warriors who remained faithful to him. They gave him the rank of brigadier general, but he seldom wore the gaudy uniform, preferring the costume of his people. In the War of 1812 he fought bravely in a number of engagements. It was not, however, as the supreme leader of a united Indian people — as he had dreamed. Instead, he was subordinate to a man he despised, the British commander, Colonel Henry Procter.

Even in war he was chivalrous and merciful. When Procter permitted the terrible massacre of American prisoners at the River Raisin, January 22, 1813, Tecumseh was not present. After Harrison repulsed Procter at Fort Meigs, Tecumseh was present, and rode up furiously to halt another slaughter of some prisoners as Procter looked on.

"Why did you not stop it before?" he demanded of the British colonel.

"Your Indians cannot be restrained," said Procter.

"Go!" thundered Tecumseh. "You are not fit to command! Go put on petticoats!"

With Tecumseh gallantly holding off Harrison's

Tecumseh The Prophet

grim advance, Procter retreated with almost indecent haste into Canada. But at last Tecumseh had had enough of retreating; he compelled Procter to make a stand on the Thames River, Ontario. The battlefield chosen was good for defense, the Indians on the right in a swampy woods, the British on the left with their flank on the river. But Harrison had 2500 men to his enemy's 1500.

Tecumseh, sensing defeat, seems to have decided to die on that field rather than live on in the bitterness of his failure. Gathering his chiefs about him, he said, "Brother warriors, we are now about to enter a battle from which I shall never come out alive."

As the fighting started, an American cavalry

charge broke the British line. Procter fled and his men surrendered.

Tecumseh, however, rallied his bravest warriors for a battle to the death. Again and again the great Shawnee, though wounded severely, furiously fought off his enemies. At last he was almost alone, like an epic hero — bleeding, gasping, but undaunted.

From one side, a soldier aimed his gun and fired. The ball passed through Tecumseh's head and killed him instantly. He died as he had wished, fighting in the heat of battle. About him lay the bodies of 23 of his faithful warriors, and many of his foes.

Tecumseh left a name unforgettable in history, but he should be remembered as one against whom the fates seemed to conspire to ruin all his great plans and hopes. His tragedy was not in his brave death, but in his failures.

He did not succeed in any of his major goals, and even before his end, his mighty dream of a universal Indian nation was hopelessly destroyed. Yet he left seeds of resistance to the white man that very soon would grow into a new Indian war — this time in the south.

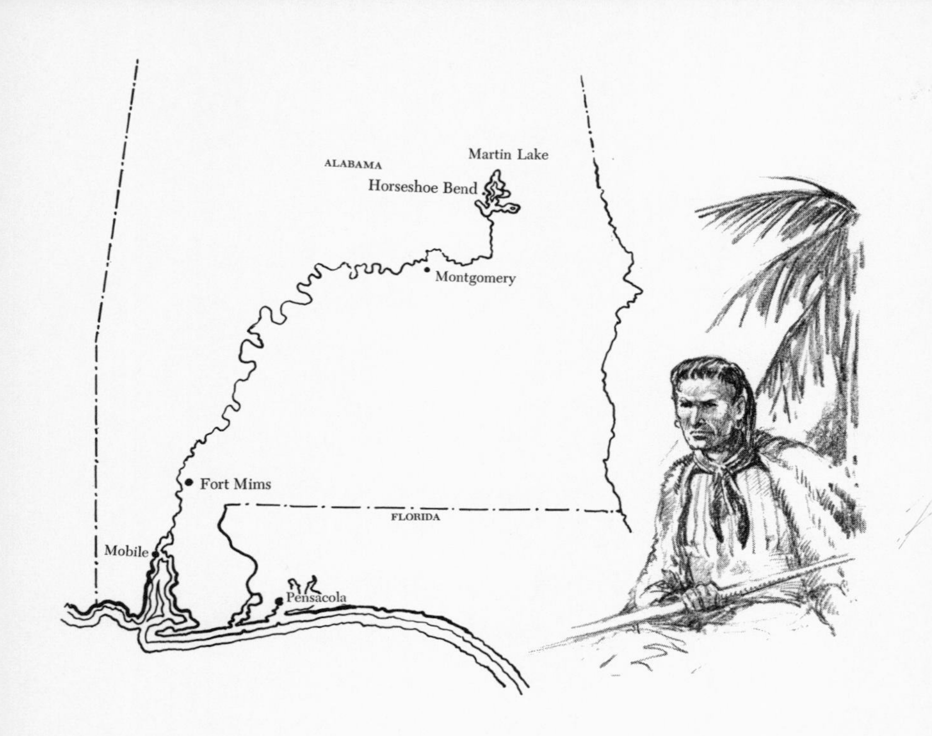

Red Eagle and Andrew Jackson | 10

SOME INDIAN WARS were justified. New England settlers fought in self-defense against Canadian Indians whom they had not harmed because those Indians were set upon them by the French. The Creek War of 1813–14 is in a similar class, but this time it was the British who incited the Indians.

The Creeks were far advanced toward civilization. They lived in permanent towns in what are now Georgia and Alabama, farmed, raised cattle, horses, sheep, and hogs, and because of their numbers —

about 30,000 — and their prosperity, were somewhat proud and haughty. Their men were taller than average European men, and some of their women were considered beautiful, even by white standards.

Indians and whites frequently intermarried. While France still held Louisiana, a certain Captain Marquand, commanding Fort Toulouse (near present Montgomery, Alabama), married, under Indian custom, a Creek girl of the Wind clan, from which chiefs generally were drawn, the descent being by the female side. A daughter, named Sehoy, was born to this couple.

Marquand was killed in a mutiny. But Sehoy, his little demi-French daughter, grew up to be famous for her beauty. In succession she was consort to a minor chief, to Colonel Tait of the British army, and finally to Lachlan McGillivray, a Scottish trader. By Tait she had a daughter, who later married Charles Weatherford, another Scotsman. Of their children the most notable was William Weatherford, known to the Creeks as Lamochattee — Red Eagle.

By this lineage, Weatherford was half Scottish, a quarter English, an eighth French, and only one-eighth Indian. Yet he was a Creek of Creeks, a thorough member of the tribe, hating the white man and preferring his Indian name. His descent through his mother, grandmother, and great-grandmother, all of the Wind clan, entitled him to rank as a chief.

Tecumseh's visit to the Creeks in 1811 made a tremendous impression on Red Eagle, and even after the failure of the Indian confederation, he was a leading spirit in urging war against the Americans. In this he was aided by British agents in Spanish-held Pensacola, who were glad to supply the Creeks with arms and ammunition for that purpose.

But the tribe was divided. At least half wanted

Red Eagle

peace. When some wild young Creeks one day murdered several settlers, the peace-party Creeks, led by Big Warrior, hunted down and killed every slayer. That widened the division in the tribe. The villages who wanted war erected poles, painted red, in their public squares. Thus they became known as "Red Sticks," to distinguish them from the peaceful Creeks.

It was Red Eagle who led the Red Sticks in a series of raids against both white and peaceful Creeks to avenge the killing of their young men. A party of emigrants was slaughtered, and some of the settlers took arms to stop the traffic in guns between the British and the Creeks.

When a posse of these settlers met a band of Creeks returning from Pensacola with their newly obtained weapons, there was a skirmish on Burnt Creek. The settlers were beaten. The Creek War had begun.

About thirty-five miles north of Mobile, Alabama, beside Lake Tenesaw, was a stockade known as Fort Mims. There, at the first alarm, most of the surrounding white population gathered. All told there were 573 persons in the fort, many of them women and children. Of these 150 were militia, commanded by Major Daniel Beasley. The commander was toplofty, arrogant, and contemptuous of the Indians. He failed to take proper precautions, even flogging a Negro slave for "spreading false rumors" when the poor fellow reported seeing many Indians in the vicinity.

For that stupidity, Beasley — and all in Fort Mims — paid the heaviest of penalties. At noon, August 30, 1813, the gates stood open while the drums beat mess call. Suddenly more than 1000 warriors, led by Red Eagle, burst from the nearby woods and sprinted silently for the fort. They were within thirty yards of the gate before Beasley himself saw them and gave the alarm. He tried to shut the massive gate — too late. Now, at last howling their war cries, the Creeks poured through and cut him down.

With that the stockade became the scene of a horrible, indescribable butchery. Men and women were cornered and killed like pigs. The few who shut themselves in the fort cabins died terribly when their refuges were set afire. In that bloody hour 437 persons, almost all the women and children, were murdered. Only 36 escaped. One, a

Negro girl, badly wounded and half dead with terror, floated downstream hidden in the bottom of a dugout canoe, and brought first word of one of the worst massacres in history.

That news, reaching Nashville, Tennessee, brought from his bed, where he lay suffering from wounds received in a duel, a brilliant and implacable fighter, General Andrew Jackson. He wasted no time. With such troops as he could gather, he marched at once for the Creek country, in spite of his physical condition.

That winter Jackson had endless trouble with his militia, many of whom left him because their enlistments had elapsed; and he fought some fierce but indecisive battles. But with a willpower few men have matched, he kept together some sort of an army, built a military road into the Indian country, and when he received some reliable reinforcements in the spring, struck Red Eagle's forces like a triphammer.

The Red Sticks had built a stronghold at Tohopeka (Horseshoe Bend). This was a peninsula formed by a wide loop of the Tallapoosa River. Across the narrow neck they constructed a very strong and high breastwork of logs. Back of this were their village and supply houses. (The place is now covered by Martin Lake, Alabama.)

Toward this fortification Jackson marched rapidly, with about 2000 men, including a regiment of regulars, cavalry led by General John Coffee, some Tennessee riflemen, Indian scouts, and a few small cannon.

He arrived at the fortification March 27, 1814. Behind their ramparts the 800 Creek warriors greeted him with yells of defiance. Their medicine men had told them the white man could not possibly capture their stronghold. But Jackson, grimly surveying it, said, "I've got them now."

He began by sending Coffee's cavalry and the Indian scouts to take positions all around the river loop, cutting off escape. Then he formed his infantry before the breastwork and told his artillery to open fire.

The cannon balls did little damage to the log defenses. Of far greater importance was an exploit by a few Cherokee scouts, who silently swam the river and set adrift all the canoes which the Creeks had gathered for a possible retreat. The dismay with which the Red Sticks learned their escape was cut off soon changed into a more desperate mood for resistance.

Shortly after noon, Jackson ordered a charge. He led it himself, riding a white horse, the regulars on his left, and the Tennessee riflemen on his right. A withering fire crackled from the Indian ramparts, and men began to drop here and there. With the figure of their gaunt, grim leader ahead on his white horse, the men never once hesitated.

First on the breastworks was Major Lemuel P. Montgomery. He was shot dead. Second on the breastworks — and first over them, fighting among the furious Creeks — was a young officer named Sam Houston. Then the whole line came tumbling over the rampart, driving the Indians back.

Still the Creeks fought desperately among the ravines, brush, and log huts of the peninsula. Houston, wounded in the thigh by an arrow, was ordered out of action by Jackson. Presently the fiery youth, only twenty years old, was seen leading a charge against an Indian blockhouse. Down he went with more wounds, from which he almost died. But so heroic was the act that it won Jackson's admiration, and from that day he and Houston were fast friends — one of America's great history-making teams.

The blockhouse was set on fire, and the last of the Creeks driven from their hiding places. Some tried to cross the river but were shot down by Coffee's men. Others fought to the death. Only a few escaped. After the battle 557 dead warriors were counted, and this did not include bodies carried away by the river. Jackson lost 49 killed and 157 wounded.

Red Eagle was not among the dead. Either he

escaped or he was absent that day. When the Creeks begged for peace, Jackson said sternly, "Bring Red Eagle here, bound hand and foot, and we will talk of peace!"

A few days later a tall, light-colored Indian, naked to the waist, presented himself before Jackson and said, "I am Bill Weatherford."

The general glared. "How dare you show yourself at my tent after murdering women and children at Fort Mims?"

"I am come," said Red Eagle, "to give myself up. Do with me as you wish."

"I ordered you brought in chains," said Jackson, "but you come of your own accord. I would gladly save your nation, but you do not even ask to be saved. If you think you can contend against me, go lead your warriors!"

The Indian drew himself up. "Well may such language be addressed to me now! There was a time when I could have answered you. I could animate my warriors in battle; but I cannot animate the dead. General Jackson, I ask nothing for myself, but I beg you to send for the women and children, who have been driven out into the woods without an ear of corn. They never did any harm. Kill *me,* if the

white people want it done!"

Jackson poured his guest a glass of brandy, and promised to help the women and children. Red Eagle promised to persuade his braves to peace.

The two men shook hands, and the Indian "vanished from the view of the astonished soldiery, a not entirely graceless figure."

The Sorrows of the Seminoles | 11

IF THE CREEK WAR was justified, that against the Seminoles was disgracefully unjust. Strangely enough, the Creeks and Seminoles were almost the same people. About 1750 part of the Creeks left the tribe and went south into Florida (then owned by Spain). The remaining Creeks called those who left *Seminoles,* or "Wanderers." They kept the same language and customs.

After Jackson defeated the Creek Red Sticks, some of them fled to these southern relatives and preached hatred of the whites. For their part, the whites — particularly the slaveholders — did not like the Seminoles, because they befriended Negroes escaping over the line into Florida.

There was trouble on the border during the War of 1812, and in 1818 Jackson, by then a national hero through his victory at New Orleans, invaded Florida. He destroyed several Seminole towns, captured Pensacola, and executed two British subjects, Alexander Arbuthnot and Lieutenant Robert Cristy Armbrister, for arming the Indians and stirring them to war.

The general was severely criticized for his high-handed actions, but he so clearly showed Spain's inability to enforce laws in Florida, much less defend it, that the United States, in 1819, was able to buy the territory for the trifling sum of $5,000,000.

No sooner had Florida become an American possession than injustices against the Seminoles began. Land sharks coveted the best of Seminole lands. Negroes were seized as slaves. One who was carried off into bondage was Che-cho-ter, a Creek woman of mixed Negro and Indian ancestry. She was the wife of a Seminole named Osceola and mother of his five children. Her husband afterward gave the whites good reason to remember their wicked act.

Under heavy pressure to force them out of Florida, some Seminoles at last signed treaties — first ceding most of their lands, and later giving up the rest, and agreeing to move as a tribe to a reservation beyond the Mississippi.

The second treaty, at Payne's Landing, Florida, in 1832, was bitterly opposed, and only seven Indians signed it. One who fought it was Osceola, a tall, erect, proud man, then twenty-nine years old, with an expressive face and light eyes that showed his mixed parentage, for his grandfather was a Scot.

Osceola was not a chief, but in the troubles that followed his fiery leadership made him the true head of the Seminoles. Asked to sign the treaty at Payne's Landing, he walked forward, drove his hunting knife through the document and into the table beneath, and exclaimed, "*That* is the only way I will sign a treaty with the white man!"

Then he walked out — to be arrested almost at once by order of General Wiley Thompson, the Indian agent. After two days in irons he did sign the treaty, but with no intention of living up to it. And when he was freed, he left a terrible threat: "I will make the white man red with blood, and then blacken him in the sun and rain, where the wolf shall smell of his bones, and the buzzard shall live on his flesh!"

His first warlike act was to shoot down a chief of his own tribe, Amathla, who sided with the whites and was returning home with money they paid him. Forbidding his followers to touch the dead man's gold, Osceola scattered it far and wide in the forest. That was in October, 1835. The Seminoles at once took to the swamps and went to war.

Osceola's second act was one of revenge. He had a personal feud with General Thompson for arresting him. On the evening of December 28, Thompson had dinner with some friends at the house of Erastus Rogers, near Fort King (Ocala, Florida).

The weather was warm, and the windows and doors stood wide open. As the guests laughed and chatted a shot rang out, and the general fell dead beside the table. Framed in a window, a smoking gun in his hands, was the fierce face of Osceola. A moment later many Seminoles leaped into the house.

Five of the guests managed to escape to the fort, but Thompson, Lieutenant Constantine Smith, Rogers, and two men named Suggs and Hitzler were killed and scalped.

On that same day, but some distance away, the first real battle of the Seminole War was fought. People had been killed in outlying settlers' cabins and a convoy of provisions and munitions was surprised and captured, with ten of the escort slain.

To punish the Indians two companies of soldiers — 110 men — under Major Francis A. Dade, marched from Fort Brooke (Tampa). A Spanish Negro guided them. It was learned later that he sent word of their route so that the Seminoles, with whom he sympathized, could waylay them.

The troops crossed the Withlacoochee River on the morning of December 28 and traversed an open barren with some scattered pines at one side and a pond surrounded by thick sedge grass on the other. Nobody thought of an ambush, for it seemed impossible for any number of Indians to hide there. Yet in the sedge lay an old chief, Mikanopy, and 200 Seminoles.

All at once the tall marsh grass beside the road literally flamed with a deadly volley. So close were the Indians to the unsuspecting soldiers that they could fire almost point-blank into them. Fully half the command was shot down at that first blast.

Dade was killed first; Mikanopy gave the signal

for his braves to fire by shooting the commander dead. In the surprise and confusion the remaining officers managed to get their men over among the trees, carrying such of the wounded as could be moved. There they beat off the first attack.

The Seminoles withdrew. Only 40 soldiers remained unwounded, but these Captain Gardiner set to work felling trees and making a breastwork, which he laid out in a rough triangle. They had raised this small defense only three logs high when the Seminoles were back, reinforced and shooting.

So heavy was the Indian fire that it was death for any defender to raise his head above the incomplete parapet. Right and left, men dropped. Gardiner fell dying, with the cry: "I can give you no more orders, lads. Do your best!"

There was nothing that they could do — but die. Before many minutes the fire from the little breastwork ceased. Over it bounded the Seminoles. Only three men, all desperately wounded, escaped by pretending death. Two died after reaching Fort Brooke. The third, Ransom Clark, lived for some time but eventually died also. It was he who told the story of the battle.

Now a desperate war was launched, a war completely baffling to the army. With their wives and children safely hidden, the Seminoles ranged at will. In the next two years they attacked settlements and military forces from Jacksonville in the north to Fort Jupiter in the south.

Osceola ambushed General Duncan L. Clinch and 700 men as they were fording the Withlacoochee. In an hour's fight the whites lost 63 men. But the Indian leader, conspicuous in a red sash and a headdress with three long feathers, was wounded. He drew off his braves. Pursuit was impossible, for the Indians alone knew the secret paths through the morasses of the swamp country.

Maddeningly, the Seminoles continued to strike, kill, and laugh at pursuit. The army imported bloodhounds from Cuba to trail them, but the watery trails baffled the dogs. A company of Indian trackers, chiefly Creeks, ran into a hard-shooting war party in a swamp and suffered so many casualties that it lost enthusiasm for the work and became almost useless. The war dragged on. Military reputations were made and lost, mostly lost.

Finally some of the Seminoles tired, among them old Chief Mikanopy. They listened to offers of money rewards if they would surrender. In June,

1837, 3000 of them had been gathered at Fort Brooke by General T. S. Jesup, ready to make the long journey to the western reservation.

On the black night of June 4, two dark figures stole into the camp of the surrendered Indians. Moving like shadows into the tent of the sleeping Mikanopy, they held bared knives over him and told him they would cut his throat if he did not order his Indians to leave at once.

Next morning when Jesup rose, happy at what he thought was the end of the war, he was dismayed to find the camp deserted and every Indian miles away, beyond pursuit. The two daring warriors who caused this evacuation were Osceola and his chief lieutenant, Coacoochee (the Wildcat).

Jesup was furious, and one can sympathize with him; but nobody can sympathize with his act of treachery that followed. He arranged a parley, under a flag of truce, with Osceola, Coacoochee, and some of their people. Believing themselves protected by the laws of the nations, the chiefs came.

Suddenly they were surrounded by soldiers with leveled guns. Outraged, astounded, they could only surrender. That act, which was denounced by right-thinking Americans everywhere at the time, forever remained a blot on the name of Jesup and on the government, which never disavowed it.

Coacoochee made a daring escape from Fort Marion (St. Augustine), but Osceola was sent for safe keeping to Fort Moultrie at Charleston, South Carolina. Brooding over his betrayal, he grew ill from loss of freedom, and at last refused to eat. He was found dead in his cell, in January, 1838.

But his Seminoles fought on. On Christmas Day, 1837, Colonel Zachary Taylor (later to be President) located a band of perhaps 300 warriors on the north side of Lake Okeechobee. He had 1000 men, but the Indians had the advantage of position, for a morass choked with sawgrass lay between.

At Taylor's command a regiment began struggling across the three-quarters of a mile of bog, men falling under the Indian fire, and frequently drowning in the water holes when wounded. At last they stopped and showed signs of retreating. At once Taylor threw in his second regiment.

Now the charge continued. By a flanking movement the Seminoles were driven from their small dry island. They lost 14 killed. Taylor had 26 dead and 115 wounded. The "victory" — if it was one — had been costly. After the battle Taylor had almost as much trouble getting out with his wounded as he had in reaching the place.

Four more years the Seminoles led the exhausted, frequently famished and fever-stricken troops from swamp to swamp, jungle to jungle, and bayou to lagoon in a fruitless chase over a region of more than 45,000 square miles. White men traveled at peril of life in interior Florida, and hundreds were slain.

At last, in May, 1841, Coacoochee was captured. Told he would be hanged unless he induced his people to emigrate, he replied fiercely, "You say I must end the war? Look at these irons! Can I go to my people — Coacoochee in chains? Never ask me to see them so. Could I go to them unchained,

they would follow me. But they will not obey me when I talk to them in irons!"

He was finally persuaded to send messengers. His people were loyal; all of his band came in. Other bands followed. By 1842 army officers believed they had shipped all the Seminoles out of Florida. They were mistaken. Seminoles remained, and not until 1844 did the last of them lay down their arms. The descendants of these still dwell, a colorful people, in the Everglades of Florida.

For seven years no more than 2000 Seminole warriors had defied, often defeated and eluded ten to twenty times their number of troops. The war cost the government $20,000,000 — four times the purchase price of Florida — besides the lives of 1500 regular troops and perhaps 2000 volunteers and settlers. And the treachery to Osceola provided a black page in American history. It was the curtain for Indian fighting east of the Mississippi.

It did not, however, end the resistance of the red man. West of the Mississippi other tribes, whose names were strange in the East — the Sioux, Cheyennes, Comanches, Modocs, Pueblos, Apaches, Nez Percés, and others — would continue the fight in future years. But the Seminole War marked the last real challenge to the encroaching whites east of that great river which was known to the Indians as the Father of Waters.

And what was accomplished? We think of America as "belonging" to the Indians before the white man came. This is true only in the sense that a very thin population of natives hunted over it and occupied it. From the wide view — the view of the human race as a whole — it is not right for a vast area of productive land to be kept as an unused wilderness. Too badly does the world need food and materials. Where they are, men will go and make that land productive, at any cost. It has been so since history began.

So perhaps the chief, and almost the only, justification of the white man's driving of the Indian from his hunting grounds is this: where once the area of the United States harbored no more than a few hundred thousand Indians, warring against each other, hunting and sometimes starving, it now supports in unequaled prosperity more than 173,000,000 people of all races — including more persons of Indian blood than were alive when Columbus first saw the New World.

INDEX